THE ROSE CROSS AND THE GODDESS

Shows how the successful search for the Eternal Feminine
Principle can provide mankind with a way out of the psychic
unbalance that threatens to destroy life on this planet.

D1615725

By the same author
EXPERIENCE OF THE INNER WORLDS
A HISTORY OF WHITE MAGIC
THE OCCULT – AN INTRODUCTION
OCCULT EXERCISES AND PRACTICES
THE PRACTICE OF RITUAL MAGIC
A PRACTICAL GUIDE TO QABALISTIC SYMBOLISM
THE SECRET TRADITION IN ARTHURIAN LEGEND

The ROSE CROSS AND THE GODDESS

The Quest for the
Eternal Feminine Principle

by

GARETH KNIGHT

THE AQUARIAN PRESS
Wellingborough, Northamptonshire

First published in 1985

British Library Cataloguing in Publication Data

Knight, Gareth
   The Rose Cross and the Goddess
   1. Femininity (Psychology)
   I. Title
   155.3'.33   HQ1206
   ISBN 0-85030-358-3

*The Aquarian Press is part of the
Thorsons Publishing Group*

Printed and bound in Great Britain

'I, King, have dealt with the gods for three generations of men, and I know that they dazzle our eyes and flow in and out of one another like eddies on a river, and nothing that is said clearly can be said truly about them. Holy places are dark places. It is life and strength, not knowledge and words, that we get in them. Holy wisdom is not clear and thin like water, but thick and dark like blood.'

Priest of the goddess Ungit
from *Till We Have Faces* by C. S. Lewis

To the memory of
Margaret Lumley-Brown
who knew about these ancient things

Contents

Part One:
The Magic Circle
Maze Dance

Man's current delusion is an over valuation of the intellect. That which has given him so much and enabled him to transform the conditions of his being by technological wonders.

Yet his inherent psychic unbalance is projected forth into his environment, that 'vegetable glass' in which he sees his own image. Half the world starves; the rich get richer, the poor get poorer. Technology, that does so much to release many from labour and fear and pain, does nothing for others, except allow them to be exploited the more efficiently.

And this applies not only to humankind itself but to the other units of consciousness that share the planet, in animal and elemental forms. Some of these man exploits shamelessly—the rape of nature with the machine. To others, the subtle Elemental Worlds, he does not even acknowledge existence, let alone rights.

Whatever man does to lesser forms of life he does to himself. As he tips the balance more and more askew with his technological contrivance, so does the day approach more quickly when his own brain children, the chemical, mechanical, electronic, sub-atomic monsters, will destroy him.

Even now, fearsome weapons of destruction are trained on every human man, woman and child, sufficient to destroy them several times over.

The fiendish ingenuity is based on intellectual limitation, fed by pride and fear. All, despite its horror and the obscene might of its destruction, is logically excused, explained and justified in the corridors of the powers of the nations.

'So far so good' is the tenor of the justifications. Words of wisdom from a man falling over a precipice, who has not yet struck the ground.

Let man, rather, discern his real predicament, and grow wings! It is really not so impossible.

In the Mysteries of the Rose Cross and of the Goddess are laid down ways to achieve the apparently impossible. They are patterns of guidance laid down by intelligences beyond the norm of human limitation; and they show a way out of the labyrinth of man's ingenious self-deception.

The Magic Circle
In the four-fold cycle of the seasons and of the day star is the magic circle made for this technology of inward flight. That is:

> Spring, Summer, Autumn, Winter
> Dawn, Noon, Dusk, Midnight.

And these stations mark the Elemental Cross of:

> Air, Fire, Water, Earth.

at the cardinal points of:

> East, South, West and North.

The symbols of these directional stations of inner space are:

> the Sword, the Wand, the Cup, the Disk.

From these four-fold properties do all the other attributes derive that form a model of the human soul and also of the Universe.

In the star stations of the Zodiac, of what we might call the Girdle of the Goddess, are further symbols of this cross. They are the Kerubic Emblems of the Vision of Ezekiel, later adopted for those of the Evangelists:

> the Man, the Lion, the Eagle, the Bull,
> or Aquarius, Leo, Scorpio, Taurus,
> the 'fixed' signs of the Zodiac.

Thus a great compendium of symbolic lore can be made, that may form the alphabet for a mode of communication between the planes. From *use* of the symbolism a language is made. But mark the word *use*. It must become a part of the fabric of one's being, by *meditating* upon the stations. This includes, but is much more than, intellectual speculation. We must read the magic circle with the feet as well as with the heart and mind.

Mark out a circle upon the ground. This act is a parallel of the original act of creation. It involves the determination of a centre and of a certain area of influence.

Take a rod or peg to hold a stable centre, and from it extend a cord. Start if you wish with the cord enwrapped round the rod as if drawing spun thread from around a spindle. Proceed, in a clockwise direction, to unwind the cord. You will find that you mark or trace out a spiral dance that culminates in a circle. Thus are you re-enacting the primal creation. Do this many times, fully aware of the significance of what you are doing. You will thus learn much of your spiritual origin and the principles of creation.

Merely to read of it is to miss the experience.
You cannot travel to market without stirring your feet.
You cannot experience reality from the pages of a book.
The pages can guide your feet. But it is up to your feet to follow.
Intellectual curiosity and impatience are no substitute for patient plodding behind the plough.
Mental speculation grows and hoes no cabbages. You learn only by doing.
If you are not prepared to learn by doing you may as well close this book. It has nothing to teach you.

The first time you perform this exercise you will be pre-occupied by physical problems and distractions. With persistence you will find that you can perform it with your inner faculties to the fore, aware of the profound significance of the pattern which you trace.

Early man spent much time and effort carving spiral symbols on rock. You will be much rewarded by spending a fraction of his time and effort carving these same symbols upon your consciousness.

You may find it worthwhile to construct a pillar as a central pole for your circumambulations. If out of doors you might utilize a tree.

These props will not be necessary after a time. You can later tread the spiral and circular path from an imaginary point. It is no less real because it is fixed only in the imagination. But initial grounding in the physical is important.

The dynamics of scale are also important. Scale is a measure of human proportion. Let the circle so traced be relative to the human form – some six to twelve feet in diameter. Certainly no less, probably not much larger. Tracing out spirals and circles on a sheet of paper is no substitute. Expression by treading is of prime importance.

How far do you really expect to travel if you will not take the first step?

When you have constructed a circle in this manner you can leave the implements of construction behind. Then, whenever you wish, you can tread the spiral and circle dance in meditation, fully aware of the profound significance of the patterns that you tread.

Develop your meditation in the following manner. Spend some time in silent contemplation at the centre point being aware of nothing but stillness and darkness. You are a being of latency, a babe of the abyss, floating in a dark warm sea of interstellar space. You see nothing about you, but you have a warm sense that somehow you are cared for. That you are not entirely alone, but are watched over, encompassed by a love you do not see or comprehend. You are drifting in a warm sea of love.

Then as if from a centre in another dimension than your own, become aware of an approaching being—a being of great light and vastness—that approaches singing and in spiral dance—like a great Catherine Wheel, or nebula. A great being who by his coming through your space attracts little beings like yourself. You see that there are already others about him in a great whirling spiral of light. You are caught up in a great positive love and attraction for this being who is like an elder brother to you, though an elder brother of vastly greater age and cosmic experience. Feel yourself caught up into his ambit, and responding to his invitation to the dance.

At this point commence your own spiral movement outward from the centre, and as you do so, be aware of being in the company of a host of others as yourself, all in the joyful train of this Great Being. As you move outward in your spiral be aware that you are proceeding through areas of space that are gradually denser—that there is a different quality of abstraction the further you approach the full extent of your circle, the Ring-Pass-Not of your system. Feel that you are proceeding through different bands of possible life expression until you reach the outer ring of the extent of the radius of your circle.

There continue to pace in a clockwise direction. Be aware that, as you revolve, the host of other sparks of divine fire, with whom you are conjoined about the Great Entity, are gradually sorting themselves into concentric bands.

Be aware now of that Great Being of light and love and power being at the centre of your circle, and of others like yourself in stately circular movement about him, at various radial distances, some moving more slowly, others more quickly, but all in stately order. See them as coloured spheres, or other geometric shapes, and be aware that you are part of a great system of ordered being—like the popular model of a solar system of sun and planets, or of sub-atomic particles about a nucleus.

As a conclusion to this meditation you may stop, face inwards and imagine at the centre, in whatever form you choose to use, the presence of God, the centre of your creation, the axis of your being. Form a loving rapport with that Being. Then turn and face the outer world across the circumference of your trodden circle and go about your daily duties.

Thus is the initial circle built up from which much else may follow. We are creating a two-dimensional spatial model of the inner universe. A model on one plane of a reality that extends into many dimensions.

The average person never dreams of these realities. It is an ignorance that is sad and poignant in individual terms. They are like children who think they are orphans because they do not recognize their own birthright. It is also dangerous to the world at large when this limited view becomes the accepted 'reality', and a godless humanity, cut off from its own roots, runs mad in spiritual darkness and blindness. When, like Oedipus it has killed its own parents and rendered itself blind.

To such, humanity seems confined on a planetary penal colony, cut off light years away from its nearest starry neighbours. In truth the universe is a loving and close family. Only loveless illusion makes it seem as it does to the scientific instruments of men: vast and lifeless. Man projects his own inner condition upon the 'vegetable' or cosmic glass about him. We hope and pray that he melts with love the confines of his prison. That he will not allow it to remain and become his cosmic condemned cell. That mankind will choose love, and live.

The Cross of the Elements

Let us learn the stations of the circle. They are situated at the cardinal points. They are modes of reality. As such they are creatures of the imagination. Yet so, indeed, far more than many realize, is the structure of the universe. This too is the projection of human imagination. Change the imagining and you change the world. The demonstration of this concept demands faith. And if demonstration is sought then faith is insufficient. An instance of divine paradox upon which all fundamental reality is based.

We have already named the four cardinal points. Locate within your room the points of East and South and West and North. Align them with a compass if you will, although this is not of prime importance; we deal with inner directions beyond the confining illusions of space and time.

In general terms, however, if the configuration of your room seems generally to agree with it, it does no harm to consider East to be more or less the direction in which the sun rises. The other directions follow from this.

The following exercises should be performed slowly, with much imagination, and many times. Indeed, as this is done so will they cease to be exercises and become living experiences, as you develop the organs of perception that go beyond the limitation of physical sense.

Yet, all that follows is based upon sensual physical reality and this is of imperative importance. If you have not your ground base of physical experience then all is a shimmering mirage, the flickering of a lantern. Think well: the physical is the end result of spiritual forces. Therefore to seek the source of those spiritual forces, the Ariadne's thread, to lead you through the psychic astral maze, must be anchored in the forms of earth. These physical forms are reflections of a spiritual reality. They are reflections of the ultimate truth beyond form. Look well into the mirror of nature to see the reflection of the spiritual stars.

No time is wasted in cultivating the world of sense. Of communing with nature. Of rising early to walk out and see the rising dawn. To lie in the noonday sun. To walk in contemplation at eventide and go abroad at midnight gazing at the moon and the starry sky. Listen to the birds, feel the breeze, smell the scents of nature, lean against the trees and feel their vitality and strength. Walk through the brooks, the dewy grass, the oozing mud, the sharp frost and driven snow, the drifting fallen leaves, the driving rain, the gentle drizzle. Learn the alphabet of nature. It is also the alphabet of the core of your being, by which you can learn to speak the language of God and the gods, of angels, elementals and justified men.

With this fund of experience, much of which you gathered as a child, learn to become like a child again, and experience with equal vividness the stations of your circle. This is the sacred dance of life.

Invocation of the East
Go to the Eastern point and face outward. Be aware of a darkened horizon across a wide plain. In the sky before you is a single light in the darkness of pre-dawn, that of Venus, the morning star. Then see the sky gradually begin to lighten to a light turquoise green. And see a smaller light, just before the sun comes up, of its companion and herald, Mercury the messenger of the gods. Then the tip of the golden disk of the sun itself begins to rise above the horizon and all is slowly bathed in red and gold, and long dark purple shadows gradually give way to increasing light. At the same time be aware of 'the voice of the day', the morning chorus of bird song welcoming another dawn. Realize too that it is spring time. See about you on the low bushes and the trees behind you the green buds bursting forth with new life. Of spring flowers shooting up sharp shafts of green through the earth at your feet. And then be aware

too of a gentle but persistent breeze upon your cheeks—for this is also the quarter that is dedicated to Air. Be aware also, with the inner eye, of little winged beings, with the appearance of nursery tale fairies but which have an ancient lordliness that comes from experience since the beginnings of time. Finally, as the sun rises above the horizon, see standing before it a great stag, with branching antlers. If you count them they number twelve and each tine, as it reflects the early morning sunlight, seems to be afire with a point of incandescent light. Imagine you have a great sword before you. See and feel its jewelled cross-formed hilt. Withdraw it from its scabbard. See its blade shine out brilliantly in the sun's light and with it salute the mighty stag, Cernunnos, and the beings of the dawn and spring. Replace the sword, and take a long bow from your back and an arrow from a quiver at your side. Fix the arrow into the string of the bow and take a long strong pull, and try to shoot the arrow over the sun. Hear the arrow buzz through the air as it leaves you and feel the slap of the string and the whip of the untautened bow and be aware of the flying arrow, a brief gleam in the sunlight, and then a quivering dark line against the azure sky, before it disappears from sight, to fall you know not where, but in the direction of your aspiration.

Be aware also of two other great figures who build at the bidding of your mind's eye. One a great winged archangelic figure who towers over the whole scene before you, winged, and robed in blue and gold, the great Archangel Raphael, bearing a pilgrim's staff and a scrip or purse containing the elements of healing.

Also, larger than human stature, the King and overlord of all the Elementals of Air, mighty Paralda. As you see him be aware of all the peoples of the element Air whirling about in a great spiral of force that is as steady as a strong breeze, and be aware of air flowing through your whole body, cleansing and purifying, blowing all dust and cobwebs of stale thoughts, feelings and conventions away.

Invocation of the South
We may now proceed to the Southern point. When practice and proficiency are gained all the four quarters may be built in imagination at one session. To begin with, however, one quarter

alone will be more than sufficient. When all are, in course of time, built with some reality in the manner described, they should be worked with in a balanced fashion. Rotating from one to another, each day, or perhaps over a longer period of a week or, at most, a month. Remember that we are building a cross that is a model of the forces of life in which we live and move and have our being. In the course of time when you are fully proficient, it can be realized and worked with, as a balanced whole.

Go to the Southern point and face outward. There be aware of being bathed in the bright sunlight of noon, the warmth of the life-giving radiation of the day-star soaking through you. See the sun a great incandescent disk, with golden rays shooting forth from it in all directions. It may take up the whole of the sky rather like the Tarot Trump of the Sun, a beaming face upon its disk in token of the fact that it is alive, a warm, sentient and conscious being, that cherishes, nurtures and loves you and all else upon the planets within its ambit, that circle it in adoration and love. You may see yourself as one of the naked children that dance within a ring in the sun's rays this side of the wall of form, with the high nodding heads of sunflowers beaming over you, reminders of the complete reliance upon the sun for birth, life and breathing by the world of animal life and vegetation. Or you may be aware of yourself as the variant of the Tarot Trump that depicts a naked child upon a white horse, carrying a banner.

That banner is the glorification of life, and may have upon it either a simple heraldic device, a red cross on a pure white ground, or alternatively be richly sewn with embroidered flowers, animals, birds and fish, a great tapestry of all created life under the sun. These various visions may be evoked either one after the other, or as alternatives on different occasions.

The horse may also appear before you as Epona, the great white mare of the hills. You may see her, perhaps in the form of one of the great chalk hill figures carved by the Celts, or those who came after even to the present time. If so, be aware of the chalk figure, coming alive, and galloping over the green hills in the sunshine. In the bright sunlight that surrounds you be aware of points of diamond light—these are the consciousness of the beings of fire, like fire-flies of the day, the salamanders, also called 'will of the whisps'. They are capable of giving great spiritual contacts for they serve the great ones at all levels of being and they are forces of transmutation and transformation behind the fires of life. Now imagine that you have in your hand a long stripped wand of hazel wood with a hollowed core through which powerful subtle forces play. Something of this may be seen in the raying points of starlight that shine from its endmost tip and can be felt in the almost animal warmth of the end that is grasped within your hand—a warmth that seems to stem from deeply banked furnace fires from within the depths of the earth, and of the quality of the deep seated fire that is within the sun. This is the planetary and solar Kundalini, the serpent power, a reflection of which you carry within the core of your aura, in the equivalent of your spinal column. Make a sign in the air in the form of a five pointed star, commencing at the topmost point and swing down right, up left, across, down left, and up to top again. This is the symbol of man, solar spirit in balanced command of the four elements. Then see yourself standing four square facing the South holding a great spear. Its haft on the ground beside your foot and its flaming point, like shining bronze, above your head. Be aware of the great rod as being a tool of control. To point and keep things at bay, or to handle virile forces, as a rod is used to stoke a furnace, or to fend off a violent creature. It may also be held two handed as a weapon of defence, fending off blows but harming none, or being used as a means of exerting pressure or holding a door as with a bolt across its opening. Be aware of your rod as an organ of control.

Then see before you, building in the sky, the red and gold fiery figure of the Archangel Michael, also armed with a long and mighty spear with which he quelled the dragon. Not only the dragon of evil as the vulgar assume but the dragon force that is the virile power of all growing life, the fires of creativity, which create destruction if let run riot but which are the fire springs of creativity and all manifest life when co-operated with and controlled. Then, associated with the Archangel, be aware of the great King and lord of the Elementals of Fire, the great fiery heat of the mighty Djinn, lord of all heat and warmth, whether of the animal warmth of the nest, the hearth fire, or the primal fire of the atom. Be aware too of the purifying radiations of heat and fire passing through you from his subjects, many of whom form a part of your being and keep your bodies alive.

Invocation of the West

Proceed to the Western point and face outward. Be aware of the soft contemplative hush of eventide, and of being surrounded by the rich gold of autumn colours and of ripe fruits and nuts, and the gathered corn and all good things of harvest home. See yourself at the border of a still lake, upon which there is scarcely a movement, save for the odd fish rising to form an eddy of ripples, or the buzz of insect life about its surface. On the horizon before you the sun, a great dull gold disk sinks towards the horizon in a soft glory of shades of crimson, and, as you watch, it disappears below the ground of the purple mountains in the far West, on the other side of the lake, whence you can see far in the distance a winding path leading up to the heights. As the sun disappears, yet still signals its presence by the afterglow of glories in the cloudbanks of the Western sky, you notice in the greening azure of the upper sky a few first faint stars, and shining predominantly amongst them, as herald of them all, the great lamp of Venus, the Evening Star. At the same time be aware of a last flicker of a point of light from Mercury, the Messenger of the Gods, and attendant of the sun, following its master below the horizon. And then be aware of the mistress of the night sky, the crescent moon, with the evening star between its horns, like a pale lantern in the sky before you.

The darkening clouds of the Western horizon almost appear to be like herds of lowing cattle, and you are aware of a great figure of a spotted cow, building over the lake before you. This is Mona, most ancient of sacred symbols.

Within your hands you find you hold a silver cup, and before you on the ground is a cauldron, simmering over a slow fire. Sweet savours are rising from it. You raise your cup towards the great beings of the West and you drink a toast to them that is almost a sacrament. Then you contemplate the rising vapours that ascend above your head in the still air from the cauldron of inspiration, that has images of nine goddesses cunningly worked about its rim.

Be aware as you do so of the great archangelic figure of Gabriel, in blue and silver, before you, bearing a great horn of annunciation, he who is bringer of tidings and visions. With him, in the lower parts of his aura may be discerned the great Elemental lord of Water, known as Nixsa. And as you become aware of him you also realize the presence of his creatures, beautiful nymphs and sirens rising from the depths of the lake, some like dolphins, others bearing pearls and sea treasures, and calling on conch horns, and you feel the purifying streams of water flowing through your being.

Invocation of the North

Now go to the Northern point of the circle and face the North. Feel that you stand at midnight, in the crystal deeps of Winter, looking at the night sky. It is the dark of the moon, or rather just past that point for a thin sliver of the new moon is visible as a shining silver line that, as yet, casts little light, so that the stars in the sky shine out as brilliant gems as if great diamonds on a back cloth of deep indigo velvet, of differing sizes and brilliancy, and some flashing or sparkling in various colours or highlights. The scene before you is illuminated entirely by the star light.

See trees and bushes before you in the landscape without their leaves, save for the evergreens, whose needle like leaves glitter with frost in the star-light like tinsel on natural Christmas trees, with highlights and reflections from the star-shine like glittering fairy lights.

Be aware of the Pole Star in the centre of the Northern sky before you, situated at the tail end of Ursa Minor, and, circulating about it, the Northern constellations of Draco, Ursa Major, Casseopia, and the house-like form of the chair of Cepheus. Learn to become familiar with the patterns of the stars; they hold the ancient starry wisdom.

Imagine that you hold in your hands a circular disk that is in fact a black mirror, of polished stone, that reflects whatever part of the sky whose image you catch in its depths, and which also imparts to you intuitively the meaning of the patterns. Then be aware that you also have a shield that on the outside is of a similar substance and which shines forth your own particular sigil that expresses the innermost star of your being, whilst the inside of the shield is like a brightly polished silver mirror, that enables you to see yourself in the utter clarity of perceptive wisdom.

Then see building before you in the landscape the figure of a great bear. Artor, standing swaying, clasping a ragged staff—a great protector of his territory and of all of his kind. Be aware that you have the status of one of his bear-cubs, a privilege that in due course of growth in your stature will lead to your taking on similar responsibilities and powers as the bear.

A great archangelic figure also builds before you, that of Uriel or Auriel the giver of wisdom, seen dark against the sky, a shadowy beneficent presence who watches over neophytes. And with him see the Elemental form of Ghob the King of the Gnomes, in the colours of Earth, that contain the olive, citrine and russet colours of a ripe apple. He is surrounded by his underground creatures, who can pass easily through solid objects and who are familiar with the mineral deeps of the earth and of the treasures and forces therein. Feel the steady warmth of the stability of Earth that holds you in a fructifying steadiness as if you were a germinating seed supported in the dark bosom of the Earth.

Working with the Circled Cross

You have now formulated the cardinal points of a circled cross, the equal armed cross of the Elements, and if you so had a mind, and the space that could be so dedicated, you might build an appropriate shrine at each of the four quarters, perhaps with a small altar containing appropriate symbolism; or also perhaps containing a seat wherein you could sit and commune with the appropriate forces and bring them through your dedicated consciousness. Just as ordinary mortals sun-bathe, as they call it, by physically opening themselves to the rays of the sun, so may you also, in balanced turn, immerse yourself in the rays of the four Elements. You might also, if you wish, have coloured robes appropriate to each quarter—though none of this is essential. The enhanced imagination, vibrating with sympathetic emotion, is the true mode of working to effect. But the ability to 'earth' these inner realities is never a bad thing, save when they become the baubles of self-indulgent glamour. Making the symbols and the regalia yourself is of greater worth than simply buying them. Although if they are indeed bought and not made, then a purchase that is something of a sacrifice is of more benefit than one that is easily afforded.

There is a tradition about the four principal symbols, that

need not be adhered to rigidly but which demonstrates their inner principles.

> The sword or dagger of the East should be earned;
> The wand of the South should be made by yourself;
> The cup of the West should be received as a gift;
> The symbolic pentacle of the North should be designed by yourself.

Thus are dedication, spiritual will, love and wisdom expressed in these cardinal symbols.

As for the colours of the various quarters, think deeply and vividly of the qualities embodied by each direction and allow the images to rise. Have the faith of your own vision in all these matters. This bears greater fruit than all the speculations of intellect. Many are the system builders, but their structures are as lifeless as a scaffold. We seek the actual realms of the evoked imagination—not the maps and travellers' tales of the analytical mind. The mind is slayer of the real: the pin that transfixes the living butterfly to the tabulated board—for its vibrant colours to slowly decay. Follow the living symbols through the meadows of inner vision as a child delighting in the random colours and smells and sounds of nature. You will find it has an inner logic and structure of its own. The principles of discovery are the same on the inner planes as they are on the outer. Simply observe. What you see and hear may amaze you.

You may stand in the centre of your circled cross and realize it as a point of balance—as a condition to which you should aspire. When you have balanced the elements of your nature as represented by the arms of the cross, then may the rose of the spirit bloom. This is one meaning of the Rose Cross.

Standing is a valid posture for those of the Western Mysteries; so also is sitting upright in a chair. A position of balanced poise is that which is sought. It brings comfort without distraction and can be held, if need be, for a long time. The legs should not be crossed, a position that is physically damaging as well as psychically twisted.

If the aura requires to be closed, that is if you wish to remain in communion with yourself, then the hands may be lightly clasped, and the ankles crossed. For general work the hands can either rest on the knees if sitting, or hang by the sides if standing. They can also be used for various gestures, of receptivity, invocation, evocation, banishing, rejection, direction, in ways that are best discovered by trial and error. Do and develop what feels right. That is the key to effective work. In the East much has been written about postures and hand and finger positions. This may be well for those who follow the ways of the Orient, but they do not necessarily pertain to the West.

Mankind, more than is realized, is an expression of that part of the Earth upon which he subsists. A rose of the West should not aspire to bloom like a lotus of the East. Though there may be rare instances of those who have such a personal destiny.

Pictures of Egyptian or Assyrian gods and goddesses give a pattern of postures for the West. A footstool of modest size may be a useful addition to raise the feet so that the thighs run parallel to the floor.

Feet on the ground is an important part of Western posture. The destiny of the soul incarnate in the West is control of the physical environment. Mark the word control and not abuse. That of the Eastern soul is more subjective. There, the feet are best raised above the base of the spine, or closely conjoined to it, so forming a closed circuit of the aura not open to objective Earth currents.

The Pillars
The concept of the Pillars is of great importance. Everything that exists to objective perception is a manifestation of forces in duality. These dual forces, in complement or vortex, are represented by two pillars.

The pillars may be pictured as silver and black, or green and gold, or of other contrasting or complementary colours. Colour symbolism is largely subjective. Its expression is a uniquely personal statement.

The forms are more objective, in their mass and space and relative position, one to another.

At root the Pillars are positive and negative, male and female, active and passive, but remember none of these concepts is synonymous with another. Each definition has its own limitations. The fundamental postulate is that each pillar is the opposite of the other, yet opposite in relatedness. As opposite as the centre and the circumference of a circle.

In terms of esoteric geometry see a point moving in free space. Left alone, it traces a line moving straight into infinity. See another force impinge on it besides the one that started its first movement. Now instead of tracing an infinite line it moves round upon itself. See it form a circle. Those two forces that acted on this point may be represented by the positive and negative Pillars. They are the polarity on one level that creates a form in another dimension.

At whatever level one views a form, it will resolve into two forces at a higher (or lower) plane of existence. These dual forces are depicted by the Pillars.

The representation of these Pillars also forms a Gate. Any two forces in complementary action define another plane of being where they are a unity. Two and one makes three. Thus the triangle is an important symbolic figure as well as the circle and the cross.

The importance of the triangle can be seen in various composite glyphs. Whether in simple terms of the Star of David or six-rayed star, or in more complex inter-relationships such as the many triads of the Tree of Life.

It will be no waste of time or effort to make two physical pillars. They need not be of massive size but should be worked upon to invest them with the dignity that the discipline and performance of painstaking and dedicated work confers.

In size they need be no broader than the human arm. In height one should be able to walk under them should a cross piece be balanced between their capitals. They need a secure base (as do all things manifest in Earth) and they may be fashioned round or square and appropriately painted.

One does not have to be a master carpenter, but all should be able to exercise care and diligence with the hands. To be able to work with simple tools is a fundamental lesson of life. The skill of a handicraft is never too late to be mastered. What is the point of trying to learn to handle the forces and forms of higher planes if one cannot cope with the elementary rules of the physical?

There is no escape in trying to flee from the problems of the physical plane before its lessons are learned. To dodge is merely a temporary expedient before an inevitable return to the problem; if not in this life then the next. Therefore cultivate work with the hands. Literally, within your hands lies the health of the soul and the manifestation of the spirit.

In olden temple days the seeker for higher wisdom had first to be a hewer of wood and a drawer of water. There is more to this requirement than simply a willingness for humble service. These acts are basic to life in the world. However exalted one's consciousness, one must have the ability to use, and even fashion, bucket and axe. They are each in their way two pillars of a very fundamental wisdom—that which cuts and that which contains—to give water and fire—the necessities of life.

The Pillars may be placed about the circle in various ways. Indeed a completely accoutred circle could be seen as a grove of pillars.

They may be placed upon each side of an altar in any quarter. Indeed one might visualize, if not physically build, appropriate pillars in such a fashion.

At the East a positive (right hand) pillar of the gold of the flecks in the rays in the sun, and a negative one (left hand) of the azure of deep summer sky.

At the South a positive pillar of the yellowy orange of flame and a negative of the crimson of a deeply banked furnace.

At the West a positive pillar of the silver of reflections on the waters, and a negative one of the deep grey-green-blue of the sea.

And at the North a positive pillar of the light green of new earth life and a negative one of the dark tones of ancient rock.

It will cultivate the esoteric sense to contemplate alternative colours for these, and various additional features that may not be practical in physical terms. For instance, see the pillars in movement within themselves. Shooting forth green buds; showing scudding clouds; in restless movement like the wind whipped sea; brilliantly sparkling with star light. It is here you may realize the powers of the imagination to be greater than those of the hands. And to see that the physical symbols are but outward signs of a real and vibrant reality that is not of their plane.

In due time therefore physical symbols may be dispensed with, but there is no substitute for working with them at first. They are tools of consciousness. With their aid far greater things may be achieved than leaving the mind untrained and unaided. 'Earthing' is also an important principle. The traditional vices of the material plane are disorder and inertia. The physical procurement of symbolic artefacts, and finding a place for them in physical life, is an exercise in overcoming inertia and creating physical order.

To create a model universe, a temple in the physical of the dynamics of the inner, is to demonstrate one's mastery over minor circumstances of matter. Such a created model may be the vehicle for profound realizations and high mystical experience. It is the dedication of a proportion of physical living space to express universal spiritual principles. It is the building of a life size talisman; a focus within the material world that will spread, on subtle levels, help and healing by its very existence.

By building this material model, you express the equilibration of the elements that make up the world. The rose of the spirit may bloom therein. By virtue of your tending this mystical garden you will be spreading a sweet spiritual fragrance.

The Altar
We have spoken of an altar at each quarter, between a pair of Elemental Pillars. This is to effect a focus of intention. In ultimate truth the altar is yourself. As you face the two Pillars you may see the altar between them and just beyond. If the Pillars were upright sides of a mirror the altar would be a reflection of your soul.

In token of this the altar is sometimes placed before the Pillars. It is then termed the Altar of Sacrifice, for it is only by sacrifice that one passes through the gateway to the inner worlds. This is a fundamental economy of nature. Just as matter can neither be created nor destroyed, but only transformed to another mode of expression, so when consciousness seeks to be raised to another dimension, it needs must exchange energy upon one level for energy on another.

In martyrdom for a cause, this exchange may be dramatic. In such a case the equivalent of an explosion—the fastest form of physical transformation. Yet all life is in a state of constant transformation in the process of growth and decay. It is likewise with consciousness.

The altar of sacrifice demonstrates that where your treasure is there will your heart be also. Time, effort, money, even friends and reputation may need to be expended in the search of knowledge and experience of the higher worlds, just as sacrifice or allocation of resources would be needed if your desires impelled you to seek knowledge and experience of another part of the physical world.

You may therefore stand in the very centre of your circle and be the focused balance of all its parts. This is a useful exercise, but a more solid expression to this intention may be given by placing an altar in the centre.

In basic form an altar is simply a table; a focus of consciousness. Its size and height are ones of convenience, practical and symbolic according to preference and circumstance.

It should be of a regular conformation, circular, square, or polygonal, and covered with a well laundered cloth, which most appropriately would be white.

The centre of the altar is a most especial part. It is the centre of your universe. Put something very special there. Perhaps a flower, or a sanctuary flame. This represents the perpetual light of the Spirit, in balanced manifest expression.

It will help us to pay attention to that central light with some small ceremony. At the heart of ceremony is spiritual intention, enacted with grace and precision.

The Central Light

Suppose the centre of the altar is to bear a simple candle. Let the stand in which the candle rests be of appropriate simplicity and dignity. Have before you on the altar three matches and a stone. The matches should be of the type that light with friction upon any surface, and of wood rather than impregnated cardboard. One match ought to be sufficient, but two others are set there in case the first one breaks or burns out before the candle is lit. Should more than three be needed then the implication is that conditions within yourself are not appropriate and some other activity should be found.

The appropriateness of creating fire by friction on actual wood should be borne in mind. Although a flame might with efficiency be produced by gas lighter it is not immediately 'fitting'. In all of this, it is not meticulous rules that we seek to provide, but a developed sense of symbolic appropriateness. We seek efficient function that is a clear expression of a spiritual intention within consciousness. It also has to be within the bounds of practicality. The latter is a containing factor. Ideally, for example, an altar flame might best be kindled by the friction of a fire stick. The rapid twirling of a rod within a depression in a surface with perhaps the use of a bow is one that epitomizes within itself the function of all four Quarters. (Bow of the East, Rod of the South, Cup of the West, Shield or Disc of the North.) However, except in highly skilled and practised hands, the length of time it would take to produce fire and the uncertainty of the operation would render it inappropriate, except perhaps in very special circumstances.

A wooden match being struck on stone is in our suggestion, a satisfactory compromise. The match should be ignited with due intention and realization of the miracle that is occurring. Were you alone in a wilderness you would the more readily appreciate the wonder of the flame, so easily taken for granted in the midst of modern civilization.

As you strike that match and bring to birth the living flame be aware that you are participating in the lighting of all the flames and fires that ever existed, from the hearthstones of the most primitive men to the great solar fires that shine upon you as stars from the deeps of the cosmic heavens. And be aware that it is all part of the single living flame, that has its originating spark in the heart of God.

In skilled and practised hands, the lighting of a match and a simple candle can bring with it reverberations and realizations of the very primal creation—of the original FIAT LUX. The power rests entirely within your own imagination and depth of spiritual intention.

As fire is struck from the stone, banish from your mind all negative doubts—about whether in fact the match will break, or whether it will fail to ignite, and so on—the demons of negativity are legion and prolific as flies. Simply *know* that you are going to create fire, that you *are* creating fire, causing light to shine where there was no light before, bringing warmth, bringing change, bringing all the necessaries of created life's expression. This is a moment of supreme affirmation and confidence. In performing this simple act in a spiritually oriented manner you are bringing profound powers of healing to your own soul. You are expressing the divine principle within your environment and sphere of influence. Your whole aura will light up, and the brighter and more vibrant your aura becomes, the greater and wider your powers for good, far beyond your immediate physical confines; they will transcend space, and even time.

If so much can be gained by such a simple act, performed with spiritual intention, think what power for good you have when you bring your spiritual will to bear, in love and intelligent activity, upon the other symbolic realities you build within your circle.

Take the flame to the waiting candle. The lighted match should take on the significance and power of a mighty flaming archangel, or even the Spirit of God, proceeding through space, to bring light and life to a new creation, waiting in deep latency. See the unlit candle, its wick and its combustible wax as a dark planet, or an unlit solar system, or an as yet uncreated soul, awaiting the touch of the Creator to bring it flaming to life, expressive with light and life and love.

In such a simple action so very much can be expressed. In the course of time and practice of this controlled and spiritual intention, think how your whole life could be transformed, however limited its outward expression might seem.

You are a creative spirit. Only choose to *be* one. Act out your noble destiny—be its current expression in the confines of hospital, prison or broken home; in overcrowding or loneliness. The greater the darkness, the greater can your light shine. Only start with the small things. Perform them in faith, and the greater will follow, as surely as noon follows the dawn, as the verdant spring the barren indrawing of winter.

The ethic of the physical plane is order. The smooth running of the 'machinery of the Universe'. Students of the Tree of Life will know what this means. But pause not over symbolic theory.

Go on to discover the *reality* of all that this means—in the spiritual magic of your circle.

Prometheus, who brought fire to mankind, was a Titan whose name means foresight. So be prepared for the consequences of your actions. You will need somewhere to place the burned out match. Let a discreet and adequate receptacle be provided. Simply to cast it aside is an expression of *dis*-order. A working for the Lords of Mis-rule, the evidence of whose presence is all about you in the world. It is perhaps only the lack of intention that prevents their engulfing the world in a sea of rubbish, of forgotten litter discarded by childish and immature spirits.

Be responsible, which does not mean be dull, authoritarian, priggish or pedantic. Think out the consequences of your actions and discharge them gracefully. Then you will be truly in a state of grace. The Lord helps those who help themselves. This is a profound truth, not a cynic's wit.

A cupboard or shelf beneath the altar surface can be a convenient repository for unwanted symbolic objects or tools of the art such as incense blocks, tapers or matches. That is, for all that is needed for the general work, yet is not to be an immediate focus of attention.

The lighting of a candle or a lamp upon the altar should be a prelude to all activity within your circle. It affirms the central presence of the spirit. It will serve to lift the mind to a higher level and prepare for the work to come.

Conversely, the extinguishing of the flame should be the last act in any work that you do. It should also be performed with intention—as of putting children to bed at night, or bringing down the curtain on a play, or placing the last full stop in a chapter of the book of life, so that all may return to rest and recuperation, for expression at another level of being, completely 'other' from that of the flame.

In so doing it is best to use the fingers to snuff out the flame. Or to enclose it in some other way. The breath should not be used to blow it out, for the breath is creative, the agency of the Word that calls forth, and so is not symbolically appropriate for the termination of expression.

This final act of extinguishing the flame should bring you back to the level of normal life experience. This is just as valid as what you have been doing, but does not have the concentrated intensity of life within the circle.

The Cycle of Time

In the magic circle, what seems so little can mean so much! When you are really accomplished in magic, all your life will be expressed with such concentration. But this is not likely to be yet. In its fullness it signifies the grade of the Magister Templi—one who is master/mistress of the temple of expressed consciousness. Deep words. Think upon them. But these early exercises express the fundamental principles, and set you, the neophyte, upon the Way. This is a way that leads to theoretical, practical, and philosophical appreciation of the principles of manifest life; and then to adepthood in serving its needs, before proceeding to higher and wider levels of mastery. Note we say higher and wider. Nothing is left behind. As it has been written, even the hairs of your head are numbered. And all is a significant part of the great dance. Your 'past', your 'future', your Eternal Now.

Past and future, in so far as they can be understood by incarnate consciousness, may be traced about the circle. Time, in truth, is a series of spirals but can be represented in two dimensions by a circular path. As will be apparent from the designation of the directional stations, East – Dawn, South – Noon, West – Dusk, North – Midnight this may be trod in a clockwise direction.

A deeper, personal application may be made by regarding these stations in terms of the pattern of the weaving of life's expression, in and out of bodily incarnation. For this purpose one may conceive a veil spread across the circle to make of it two semi-circles. In this case the Westernmost half is that of manifest physical life; the Easternmost half of discarnate life—of so-called 'death'. (Though denizens of that world might, more justly, use that term to describe constriction into the limiting forms of matter.)

If one has a central altar in place, about which to revolve, then two gateways may be conceived, to South and North of it. The Gate of the South is that which leads from inner world to outer world—the Gate of Birth, or Gate of the Womb. The Gate at the North is that which leads from outer world to inner world—the Gate of Death or Gate of the Tomb (Figure 1).

It may be helpful to fashion two sets of Pillars, one for each Gate, particularly if a physical veil be incorporated. A light rod

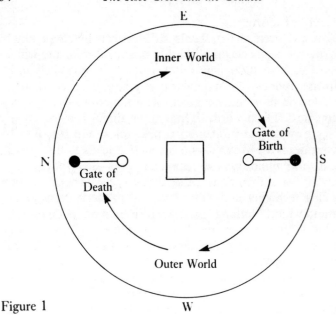

Figure 1

may be laid transversely across the top of each set of Pillars, above head height. This can be firmly affixed with small eyelets or hooks, and have a thin muslin veil hanging from it, in two separate pieces, so that there is a divide in the centre through which one may pass. Alternatively a hanging bead curtain may be utilized, of appropriate colour. Precise detail is left to individual taste and ingenuity, but dignified simplicity is the criterion. A simple blue-grey veil is as effective as an ornate curtain embroidered with complex symbols of birth or death. The latter can readily and effectively be provided by the imagination, using for its basis the simple general purpose symbolic furniture of the physical level.

Now, as an exercise, we may proceed slowly to circum-ambulate the circle, in a clockwise direction. Starting from the East, spend some time at that Quarter meditating upon your own central core of being, and conceive the idea and desire for physical expression.

When this is assimilated, very slowly proceed towards the Gateway of Birth at the South. Feel yourself descending the planes of intuitive, mental and emotional modes of expression until you feel the enclosing instinctual, etheric and physical warmth of the womb about you, just prior to your passing through the veil between the Pillars, which is the actual moment of birth. You may pause here to meditate upon the opportunities and destiny afforded by the chance of a physical life.

Now, in slow procession from South on to the Western Quarter feel the forces of growing maturity. The gradual acquisition first of the control of the interpretation of the data from the senses—the meaning of weight, distance, colour, perspective, temperature—all that the adult so easily takes for granted. Evoke the wonder of childhood, the great zest for experience. Then a coming out of the dream world of the fantasy of games, towards adolescence. The dawning of the expression of the mating urge; the experience of human polarity away from the parents onto one of your own generation of incoming spirits.

At the Western quarter you should pause. Feel yourself as a mature human being, at the peak of outer life expression. This is the polar opposite to the starting point of establishment in the life of the unmanifested spirit. This is a most important position which, if you are young, (say under thirty-five) and have not yet achieved, you should earnestly aspire to do so. It is the natural expression of the intention of the current incarnation. If one is not seeking greater material life expression at this time then the reason may be a reluctance to manifest—a seeking of a way of escape from destiny and karma by short-circuiting back to the inner worlds, through the apparent escape route of esoteric study and practice. This intention, despite its high destiny, is in fact no other than a reversion to the fantasy worlds of adolescence and childhood, or a prolonged emotional dependence on surrogate parents. At the Western quarter is the appropriate place to rest and meditate deeply upon these matters: on how you are best expressing your inmost powers in the world about you—to associates, family and friends. Try to descry what was and is your spirit's aim in incarnation. How well you have achieved, are achieving or propose to achieve this life expression.

Past the nadir of the West, and proceeding to the North one becomes increasingly reflective about the purpose of incarnation. There comes a gradual appreciation of the strength of the inner forces of the soul as the more overtly physical forces wane, with life expression fully established on Earth. This is not a period dominated by forces of ossification and decay even if many human beings allow it to become so. It should be the balanced expression of a natural process whereby the incarnate soul, as it approaches the Portal of Death, concentrates more on the inner forces. In physical terms this process commences more strongly after the menopause. With advanced physical years the soul looks back, often with enhanced detailed memory, over the lessons learned in the process of incarnation. This assessment is a necessary and preliminary part of the dissolution process. An aspect of this is embodied in the tales of the events of past life reeling quickly before a person faced with sudden death. The natural process is at a more leisurely pace, and the more fully it is achieved in the incarnate body before death, the less will the soul need to tarry on the other side of death—in the condition sometimes called the Judgment Hall of Osiris. It will be able the more easily to proceed through the progression into the higher heaven worlds, or to take up dedicated service, for a period, from the other side of the Veil. It is to aid this process that is one of the objects of the well known esoteric exercise of visualizing the preceding day's events, in reverse flow, each evening before falling asleep.

At the Gateway between the Pillars at the North be aware that your passing through is the moment of physical death. This should not be accompanied by feelings of grim foreboding or by melodramatic imaginings. It should be affirmed as a natural and peaceful passing from one plane of expression to another. Nevertheless, it is not a light step and here is an appropriate place to reflect upon the Mysteries of death; and a recitation or contemplation of requiem prayers for the dead, visualizing yourself in that position, is no bad thing.

The contemplation of one's own death is an important part of many systems of religious observance the world over, and also of systems of esoteric training. The reason is perfectly obvious. It is preparation for a natural and inevitable process; of a movement in the soul. It is an important element in the process of Mystery Initiation, which we shall proceed to examine in later pages. It is important in preventing pathologies of the newly dead, of their trying to resist the process, and becoming to a greater or lesser extent earthbound. At worst, such can be virtual vampires of the living, clinging to a wraithlike semi-existence, utilizing, not blood as in the Dracula legend, but the emotions and animal magnetism of former friends and relatives—until such time as they are forgotten on this Earth and have no choice but to move on. The soul who cannot proceed at this stage is in a similar but converse condition to the one in life who strives to remain in the fantasy world of childhood or youth.

Past the Northern Point of the Gate of Death, proceed slowly back toward the East, becoming conscious of ever greater expansion, lightness, and light. There should be a sense of a 'coming home', bearing all the realizations and experience of a life in incarnation, back to the Shining World of the great company of free spirits about the Throne of God, or however you best conceive the ultimate heights of the inner worlds in your present limited physical consciousness.

This may bring the exercise to completion; or you may proceed round the circle again a number of times. Remember in this exercise, as in life, of which it is a condensed model, they do best who make haste slowly.

A Model of the Universe

We have now fashioned a two-fold artefact, in physical expression and in consciousness. This is the means of considerable development and extension of awareness into the inner realms of form. Remember, 'form' in its true sense, is not the external appearance of things, but the subtle inner matrix, or series of matrices, that determines external shape or manifestation.

What we have fashioned is a working model of the principles of form. The archetype upon which all archetypes are based.

We have expressed the inmost dual polarity that is inherent in the manifestation of a point, moving in space in spiral fashion, eventually to consolidate expression in a circle.

That duality is now expressed on a lower plane in the static and the dynamic elements of our construction. That is in a circle and a cross. The cross represents a static matrix of energies, the circle a dynamic expression of energies within that matrix. Both circle and cross are expressions of the initiating, creative spirit that is represented by the point at the common centre of both cross and circle.

That central point is also expressed as an altar, and therefore another dimension of the cross might be envisaged. This would not necessarily be in a third spatial dimension but in a dimension in consciousness, running between the initiating creative spiritual spark and the actual physical altar. In symbolic expression of this a 'perpetual lamp' is often hung high over an altar. One may observe this in certain churches. And the altar is often also a formal four-square object. In the Masonic tradition which derives from the ancient Mysteries, it is usually in the form of a double cube. That is, a solid figure with a square top, and twice as high as it is broad and long. This form contains, in geometrical symbolism, the figure ten in the number of its square faces (two to each rectangular side and one each above and below).

On the Tree of Life of the Qabalah it is expressed as the all containing universal spark—a perpetual uncreate flame of divine self-expression at Kether, the Crown of all—and the final multi-dimensional form expression in Malkuth, the Kingdom, or Bride.

The altar usually stands between black and silver Pillars. They also are to be found associated with the Tree of Life. They represent the loom of creation—the positive and the negative poles whereby intermediate expression between the highest and lowest is formed.

We have in this dual polarity, of lamp and altar, and dual pillars, another form of the cross. This is the cross of manifestation upon which the spirit performs its circular serpentine, spatial or labyrinthine dance.

In masonic symbolism this duality is expressed by the square and compass. The square marks out the cross; the compasses the circle. This finds another expression in the heavens and the earth. The heavens are associated with circular movement, for that is what the stars describe to all who watch them from the Earth. The Earth is associated with the straight line—the measuring out of land—and the straight line that is given by a plumb bob or pendulum, or a falling object, that by the force of gravity makes a direct path toward the centre of the Earth.

It is now our task to elucidate how the circle of life and the cross of initiation may be used to open consciousness to other realms of expression of spiritual beings.

We might use the analogy of an electrical generator. This is a device for generating electrical potential (i.e., power) and movement (i.e., current). In a similar way the interaction of circle and cross is a device for generating psychical power and flow of force (Figure 2).

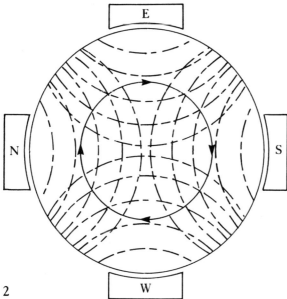

Figure 2

The electrical generator works on the principle of two coils of wire, one that is fixed (called a stator), and one that rotates within it (called a rotor). Similarly our four-fold cross is the stator, or fixed part, of our psychical generator; our circle is its rotor, or moving part.

An electrical generator works on the principle that a coil of wire moving within a magnetic field will have an electrical current induced within it. The magnetic field is provided by the stator. Similarly the four points of our cross are rendered psychically magnetic. This is achieved by the body of symbolic meaning that we confer upon them.

Thus, within this psychic magnetic field, the movement of an open consciousness will have a psychic current induced within it. This you should have proved to yourself by the exercises so far described. That is, first by the vivid building in the imagination of a complex of symbolism at each of the four quarters. Secondly in the physical process with receptive consciousness of treading around the circle.

This movement should have induced various realizations within you. Or evoked various images that might be expressions of a higher reality—tentatively glimpsed. Or flashes of memory or fore-knowledge of other incarnations. If you have not achieved any of this then more simple practice is needed.

This clockwise circumambulation is the simplest form of movement within our circled cross, but there are other movements for other purposes that are developments from this.

Musical Symbolism
We can at this point introduce another mode of symbolic expression, that of sound, for the circle and the cross can also be expressed in terms of acoustics.

In the rituals of a certain Order, the Magus of the Lodge states that each of the Officers represents 'a note in the chord of the ritual', and the Magus, by contacting each officer, then proceeds 'to set that chord vibrating'.

That chord we may derive from the harmonics of a vibrating string. The principles apply equally to a vibrating column of air, as in a wind instrument. For the sake of simplicity we will confine our remarks to a string. This was the device used by the Pythagorean philosophers to explain their philosophical number system.

If a string is plucked, and set into vibration, it will emit a note. If we then halve the length of the string, we find we have the 'same note', but at a higher pitch. Similarly if we were able to double the length of the string the note would again be 'the same', but at a lower pitch.

In the tonic solfa system, if our original note was *doh*, then halving the string gives us *doh* at the top of the scale, and doubling it would give us another *doh* at the bottom of the scale.

This is usually called being an 'octave' higher or lower. But to talk of octaves, or scales, is to assume too much at this point. The scale we are so accustomed to is but a local convention. Other civilizations have other scales which are just as valid. Indian, Chinese, Islamic, and European music sound different because they use different conventions. European music happens to use a scale of eight notes, hence the use of the term octave. This is not however a universal law. And even some European folk music uses a scale of six notes only.

The ancient Greeks were therefore more accurate in calling the space between the reappearance of a note at a lower or higher pitch as a 'diapason'. This distance in pitch, or diapason, can be divided into as many divisions as we choose. There are however certain natural divisions based on whole number divisions of a string. We have already discovered the importance of dividing or multiplying the string with the whole number 2.

By transforming a unity into an equal duality, we have created a diapason, an upper and a lower limit wherein a complete range of musical expression may be developed. This we can make the basis of another model universe, but in terms of sound rather than space.

We may now extend the model by introducing the number 3. If we take one third of the length of the string we strike a new note, that falls within the limits of the diapason. This new note differs from the fundamental note that defines the top and bottom of the diapason, yet it has an intimate feeling of relationship to it. It is, for this reason, in musical theory, called the 'dominant' note in the scale. The relationship should be experienced by the ear; it is the feeling of relatedness between *doh* and *soh* in the tonic solfa system. The whole of the Western system of musical keys is based upon this relationship between 'dominant' and 'tonic' note, and the 'cycle of fifths'.

This takes us into areas of musical theory which need not immediately concern us, although no time is wasted in acquiring the necessary technical knowledge to research further into this symbolism, which is intimately associated with the quality of numbers. The art and science of sonics is in fact the real basis of any system of numerology.

For our immediate purpose it is sufficient to say that the initial division of a string by whole numbers brings about particular fundamental soul experiences. And this forms the basic structure of a *musical* harmonic system, which may also be used to form the basis of a *magical* harmonic system.

Dividing a string by 2, we get the so-called octave, or the same note at a higher mode of manifestation. In tonic solfa this will be high *doh*.

Dividing the string by 3, we get the dominant note of any scale that one may choose to construct within the diapason of low and high *doh*. This is the so-called 'fifth', or tonic solfa *soh*.

If we divide the string by 4, we find a repetition of the tonic note at a yet higher arc; for a quarter is a half of a half, and we have introduced the principle of 2 again, in a different mode, or at a higher power (2×2 or 2^2). This would give us the higher *doh* above high *doh*.

If we divide the string into 5 we get another important note. This is generally called the 'third', or in the tonic solfa system, *me*. An important quality of this note is that it can manifest in one of two ways, each of which gives a different quality of feeling. In conventional musical terms this is called the major or minor mode. And, in very simplified terms, a piece of music will sound bright or sad according to whether the third note of the conventional scale is in the major or minor mode. (In the minor mode the 3rd is flattened.)

In symbolic terms of Pythagorean mathematics and musicology this dual mode of expression introduces the principle of polarity at a new level of expression. It is analogous to sexual and other expressions of polarity in manifestation.

Division by 6 need not detain us here. It is important philosophically in that it is a combination of the powers of the 2 and the 3. It will indeed produce a dominant note a whole scale higher. This is what might be expected from the principles of duality and triplicity combined. Harmonious expression on a higher arc.

We bring our investigation to a close by dividing the string by 7. This introduces a new quality that produces a note that is not found on our conventional scale. The principle of the number 7 throws out the balanced expression of the senarius (i.e., the numbers 1 to 6), and introduces a new quality that is outside the previously established conventions. These conventions, if they were to act alone, would simply produce ever repeating regular patterns. The 7 introduces a slightly jarring element into this infinite regular system and breaks it up into many possibilities of individual self-expression.

In musical terms the new note thus formed approximates to a flattened seventh, or a note midway between *lah* and *te* in the tonic solfa system. It does not have an entirely unpleasant sound, and may be found in natural expression in various forms of folk music.

In applying harmonic principles to the magical circle we select certain of these principal tones in much the same way that a bell is made to resonate to different harmonics of its fundamental strike tone through its shape and design. The magic circle might indeed be envisaged as a kind of psychic bell, that chimes forth at many inner levels.

In technical musical terms the four points of the circle may be described as making up a dominant seventh chord in the Dorian mode. To simplify and particularize this description: the East resounds forth the key note; the West the 'fifth' or dominant'; the South the 'third' in its flattened mode; and the North the 'seventh', also in its flattened mode.

Thus if we make the keynote of the East the tone C: then the other notes are E*b* in the South, G in the West, and B*b* in the North. The flattened modes of South and North are chosen as being more natural. When skill is acquired in the use of this system, and appreciation of the subtlety of its possible extensions, then for particular occasions other modes may be used.

To keep matters simple, it is sufficient to associate the appropriate notes we have named with the appropriate quarters. This will provide a kind of musical magical shorthand. We can by these means encapsulate the principles of different ritual patterns by means of a short sequence of melody based on this magical harmonic structure.

It is on these principles that legends on the mighty effect of words of power are based. These basic facts are indeed the foundation on which may be reconstructed the art of mantic chanting. An art almost lost to the West but that has remained developed in the East, notably in Tibet.

Different ritual patterns may be described along lines that are similar to the way that a chime of bells is worked out, as a series of permutations. Thus:

C,	E*b*,	G,	B*b*,	C	E.	S.	W.	N.	E.
C,	B*b*,	G,	E*b*,	C	E.	N.	W.	S.	E.
C,	G,	E*b*,	B*b*,	C	E.	W.	S.	N.	E.

Note that in all of these combinations we are commencing and ending the sequence at the Eastern quarter. This is because it is from this Quarter that control is usually effected. Other combinations can be developed, using the centre as a point of control but the principles are best enunciated in the first instance by the patterns above. There is indeed considerable scope for further individual research and discovery once the basic principles are understood and experienced.

E – S – W – N – E
This is the pattern of circumambulation in a clockwise direction around the circle and is a way of raising power, particularly when there are participants seated around the circle contributing their psychic force by their presence and active participation in building, in the imagination, the images described. The raising of power can be conceived symbolically as the raising of the keynote of the East an octave at each circumambulation. This in melodic symbolism could be described as an upward movement of three octaves—C, Eb, G, Bb, C Eb G Bb C' Eb' G' Gb' C"

E – N – W – S – E
This is the counter pattern to the above, and useful for closing down power at the end of a working by anti-clockwise reverse circumambulations. The psychic power that has been raised is thus given back, enriched, to the participants. Melodically, this movement, with its inherent force flow and resultant power level in the circle, can be described as:
C" Bb' G' Eb' C' Bb G Eb C Bb, G, Eb, C,

E – W – S – N – E
This is the general direction of force flow throughout the circle when the stations at the quarters are manned by responsible officers. Power comes in from the East by the principal polarity line running East – West from the officer of the East, who is the link with the inner beings behind the working. It flows to the officer of the West who acts as a focus for the corporate entity of all present in the physical circle. The force then circulates round to the Officer of the South who mediates it in love to the rest of the group. In workings where there are just the three principal

officers, as in those deriving from the Masonic pattern, the tradition is to have the neophytes seated opposite him in the North so that a particular force flow may be set up toward them. This may be assisted by a Novice Master seated with them in the North. From this point, which is the bottoming of the inner force, it returns to the Eastern office whence it originated. In its simplest expression this may be described in the melodic sequence C' G E*b* B*b*, C.

This would seem to represent a constant lowering of force but the method of working brings force through from the East and sets up higher harmonics from 'beyond the veil' so that what in effect happens is a general raising of levels. In practice, once the primary circuit is set up, the force will flow out from all officers; with its ultimate derivation being beyond the East on the inner, so that the whole pattern resembles a figure of 8; the Magus of the Lodge, in the East, being at the point joining the two circles of the inner and outer worlds.

The Magus thus forms a dominant to a higher key note on the inner. We may imagine that when the 'note' of the officer of the West is vibrating it stimulates the sounding of the Eastern Office of the inner Lodge. Then when the force proceeds to the Southern Officer and his note is sounded, a resonance is formed with the corresponding office on the inner; and likewise with the note of the Northern Office. We have then a situation best described by Figure 3 over the page.

By these means a great chord is formed and the original key note is resonated at an upper and lower level from the original sounding.

There is room for considerable research and experiment along these lines with various other permutations of force flow and their harmonic and melodic equivalents, but this is a specialism that we cannot consider here.

We must proceed to a consideration of the centre which is the vortex that is formed by the spinning circle of form expression.

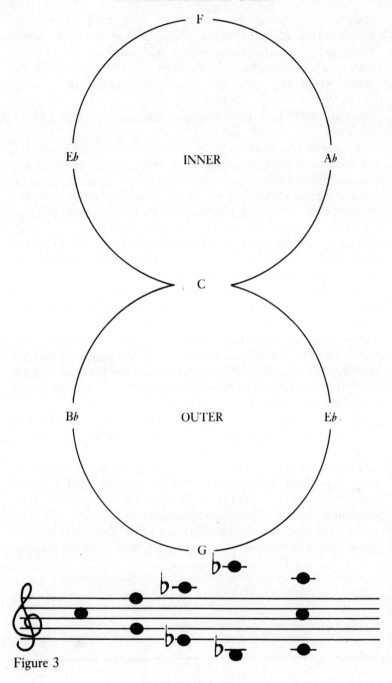

Figure 3

Part Two:
The Heroic Quest for
the Hesperides

The dynamics of the circled cross are, comparatively, at a superficial level of form expression. Although much can be achieved by exercises constructed around their Elemental principles they are but a preliminary to a more powerful, deeper mode of working, discovery and expression. This is brought about by concentration upon the centre; that which is concealed by the symbol of the crucified rose.

As should be apparent, it is of no small significance that the magic circle of life expression was derived from a central initiating point in the first instance. The same could be said if we were to extend the spatial symbolism into that of a three-dimensional sphere or any other regular solid. Indeed the symbolic importance of the Platonic solids is their adherence to the geometric principle of equal distance of all spatial outer expression from the centre.

In a more figurative mode of symbolism the magic circle could be envisaged as a shallow bowl of petals, so becoming a lotus or a wild rose. And this line of symbolic mentation that extends from geometric abstraction towards patterns in plant life forms may, by further logical extension, lead us to anthropomorphical symbolism, whereby human figures are used to represent the various forms of spiritual life expression.

In this way god forms, angelic, or elemental representations in human shape, are formulated at the Quarters. Similarly, in the centre, we may form a representation of the spirit of the rose. This would be a perfect human form of spiritual expression in the lower worlds. This is, most appropriately, the form of the

Goddess; she who sits at the centre of the wheel of life experience, spinning the thread of life and weaving it into the fabric of the worlds of form.

This is an image of extreme profundity. The Goddess appears in various forms and guises in different mythologies. And particularly in the most ancient ones where, through the overlay of later mythological and religious development, she may often appear in threatening guise.

For example we may cite the Titanic gods of the ancient Greeks. These were the gods who ruled before the reign of Zeus and the other Olympians. We glimpse an ancient matriarchal scheme of working that pre-dates the patriarchal systems of the historical period.

All this is part of a natural process of evolution of consciousness. Mankind on the cycle of life expression needs to proceed from dependence on the mother to independence based on imitation of the father. This process of childhood and adolescence in human social terms may be read in the pre-historic and historical phases of our epoch.

The time has now come when man, grown to psychological maturity, as his god-like powers over nature begin to demonstrate, must needs express his maturity by coming to terms with the feminine that he has rejected and repressed. The adolescent dreams of power and domination, the equivalent of the immaturities and inadequate sexual assumptions of a 'girlie' magazine, must give way to an appreciation of reality. The bride of mankind is the Earth. She is not an inanimate object whose body is there to be exploited in a mechanistic rape.

It is therefore of paramount importance that mankind realizes the inner nature of the Earth, and comes to terms with the profound and beautiful reality of the Goddess. This is more demanding, yet infinitely more fulfilling in every way, than the fantasies and fears of immaturity.

In commercial society these immaturities in the individual are pandered to by the degradations of the pornographic peep-show or the ministrations of the whore. It is not for nothing that the great image of iniquity in the Book of Revelations should be the Whore of Babylon. This is not a real entity, unless mankind chooses to make it so. Even then it is but a hellish travesty of true reality. The form is the mirror image of mankind's perverted desires. Its function is to disgust with the images of self-revelation. The whore is an expression of fulfilment for a particularly low level of desire. The conversion of Mary Magdalene from harlot to saint is found not so much in herself, as in man's attitude and need for her. The Whore of Babylon may then become the New Jerusalem, decked as a bride for her husband. The Earth also will cease to be seen as a lump of inanimate matter but recognized as a great heavenly being of wondrous love and beauty.

This is a meaning of the alchemical statement that the prime material of the Stone of the Philosophers is so commonplace as to be ignored. It is also the meaning of the prophetic statement that the rejected stone shall be the key-stone of the temple.

Perseus and Medusa

The most ancient feminine powers and man's relationship to them are enshrined in the story of Medusa. This is, in turn, a part of the myth of the hero Perseus, the characters of whose story are to be found in the constellations of the Northern Sky (Perseus, Andromeda, Cepheus, Cassiopeia, etc.) rotating round the Pole.

In ancient times, almost beyond the dawn of memory, there was said to be a beautiful garden far, far, in the West. There a magical orchard grew, with an especial tree from which golden apples could be obtained. This was the Garden of Hesperides.

The especial tree was guarded at its root by a serpent. And the way to it, which was across a dark and deep underground sea, was guarded by three sets of sister goddesses. From very ancient times the goddess has been associated with the number three, and here we have this principle concentrated in power, by the three sets of sisters three: the Naiads, the Graiae and the Gorgons. It is to each of these in turn that Perseus goes for assistance in his hero's quest.

It will be useful to summarize his story, for it has significance in many areas of neglected wisdom tradition.

Perseus is the son of Danäe. She who was coupled by Zeus in the form of a shower of gold whilst confined in an underground chamber. She had been entombed by her father, who feared that she might bear a son inimical to him.

In this we see an ancient form of divine kingship whereby the reigning king was sacrificed for the coming of the next. These are the hallmarks of a matriarchal society, at one with the Earth, the old king merging with the Earth in burial, for the good of the land and his people.

In the story of Danäe's father, Akrisios, we find the heinous example of one who attempted to evade his divine responsibilities by entombing the holy maiden to prevent her bearing the next divine king. However, such ancient custom, founded upon profound inner realities, is not so lightly set aside. Danäe in fact conceives a divine child without the need of impregnation by a man. Perseus is one of the virgin born.

When the child is born, mother and child are confined in a chest, or ark, and set adrift on the sea. A direct act of killing either by human hand would be too blasphemous to contemplate, but giving them over to the hands of the gods in this way is an attempted compromise whereby, it is hoped, the guilty will not have actual regicide and deicide upon their hands, and the victims will be taken back to their place of origin in the kingdom of the gods. In notable cases that have been enshrined in myth, such as this story of Perseus and Danäe, things do not work out so easily as this. The divine destiny has to be worked out to the full on the physical plane and the cosmic balance, tampered with by men's fear or ambition, set aright.

Danäe, with her shining divine child in the dark ark on the tempestuous sea, prays to the gods for succour, and they are discovered and rescued by a fisherman. No ordinary fisherman this, for Diktys, the 'net man', is of noble lineage. On one side he descends from Poseidon himself, the great god of the sea. In another tradition from Danaos, one of the mighty twin sons of Belos, (the prototype of the Phoenician Baal), and in another tradition from Io—the feminine counterpart of Prometheus, an ancient form of the goddess who predates even the Egyptian Isis. In short, Diktys might justly be called a Fisher King.

This ancient link with the later Grail legends is enforced by the similar tradition that, like the Grail King, Diktys has an evil brother, Polydyktes, (whose name means 'receiver of many') and who is King of the Underworld. By ancient right, whoever was caught in the net of Diktys became also the prey of Polydyktes. In other words, they embody an ancient teaching of the concept of free spirits being caught in the web or net of space-time, and the cyclic wheel of death and rebirth. Danäe herself becomes a captive of the King of the Underworld, but Perseus, the divine child, remains a ward of Pallas Athene, the goddess of wisdom.

When Perseus grows to maturity, the King of the Underworld throws a banquet. In accordance with ancient custom the status of those invited is assured by the fact that each has to give a horse to the host. Perseus is unable to meet this test of status but announces that he will enable himself to qualify by presenting Polydyktes with the head of the Medusa. In ancient times she was considered to have the body of a horse, and indeed was originally a mare, who mated with Poseidon himself in the form of a stallion. Perseus undertakes this quest as a means of bringing release for his mother.

In this we see a crisis point at a stage in the evolution of consciousness. It is the point where dependence upon the mother has to give way to assertion of independence. This occurs in the process of growing to maturity in all human individuals, and has its equivalent in the puberty of the human race. This is the dynamic behind many of the hero legends. The hero is one who is compelled to assert himself, to prove his individual worth by the performance of certain tests, or a quest.

This is particularly relevant in the case of Perseus, for it will be seen that achievement of this state of psychic independence will also be a release *for* the mother. On the other hand, failure to win free of the maternal influence, or mother's aura, will produce that petrification of the will that is so graphically described in the imagery of the Medusa's look that can turn her victims into stone. She is the terrible possessive mother, in this aspect. The spider woman who sucks the souls of her victims and renders them dry desicated shells. These victims are her own children.

In later legend Perseus was helped in his quest by the god Hermes who lends him winged shoes so that he can leave the island upon which he is confined. This island is an image of the physical world as defined by the outer senses; and the winged shoes confer the ability to walk the sky-ways of inner reality. This assistance from the god of travellers, magic, books and learning is valid enough symbolically but is a simplification of the original tradition that Perseus received this assistance from the Naiads, whom he visits under the instruction of Pallas

Athene, the goddess of higher wisdom.

The Naiads gave him three gifts necessary to his task: winged shoes, the cap of invisibility, and a wallet to contain the Gorgon's head.

The Naiads dwell in a cave in a mountain, an image that we shall encounter more than once. They are of the class of being known more generally as Nereides or water nymphs, of whom there are many, all daughters of Poseidon the god of the sea. However whereas the Nereides were creatures of the great waters, the Naiads were associated with inland water sources, particularly fountains.

In Arthurian legend the occurrence of a beautiful lady at a fountain is almost commonplace in the introduction to a story of inner adventures and enchantment. In the subjective economy of things such a symbolic scene represents a power point in the aura. These are known in the East as chakras. They are upwelling life-giving force centres from the depths; sources of kundalini or the life force.

This is a specialized attribution of their nymph like nature. In general terms nymphs were associated with the sexual creative function. Let us quote Kerenyi *The Gods of the Greeks*: 'The word *nymphe* meant a female being through whom a man became the *nymphios*, the happy bridegroom who had fulfilled the purpose of his manhood. The term could be applied to a great goddess as well as to a mortal maiden.'

And further: 'Three appears to have been their basic number, the number of the Graces and of the other well-known Trinities, all of which imaged the dispersed form of a great Threefold Goddess ... Hermes, their constant companion—often in the presence of Pan—represented the male fourth beside the female Trinity.'

It is relevant at this point to mention the further fact that the nymphs were particularly associated with trees and sacred groves—an important attribution that we shall again meet with more than once. Also that they are associated with counterparts representing male force in the form of the satyrs, or *silenoi*. Many of these were present, it is recorded, on the occasion when Danäe and the infant Perseus were rescued in their ark from the sea by the Fisher King.

Again, from Kerenyi: 'such beings ... were called, in an

ancient Peloponnesian dialect, Satyroi, "the full ones": a term descriptive of their "abundant", and therefore sexually excited condition. This was the more general name for them. "He-goats" who played the same role ... were also called Satyrs. The word *silenos* was also connected with such dancers, who in this role appended horses' tails to their persons. Silenoi, creatures with pointed ears, hooves and horses' tails, but in other respects in human-phallic shape, with snub-nosed faces and unruly manners, had the same privilege, of presenting themselves in the guise of a troop of male deities, as was possessed by the Satyrs.'

We see a certain connection with the fact that the Medusa was once a mare, and with the equine theme in the banquet given by Polydyktes, which initiated the Perseus quest. The symbolism of the horse is connected with the sexual energies, in the sense that their full expression is the mark of the mature human being. This signifies a spiritual maturity—the full expression of the spirit in polar relationship through all levels of form life.

From the Naiads, Perseus gains the powers necessary to approach the inner power sources. This is to be expected in that they are guardians of power sources—or fountains—in their own right. The winged shoes and the cap of invisibility are the powers of travel in the Imagination Body untrammelled by physical form; and the wallet for the Medusa's head is the ability to act objectively, or with power, upon those levels, rather than as a mere observer.

Next Perseus visits another three-fold sisterhood, the Graiae. These were located in the Underworld rather than the half-way condition of a cave in the overworld. Daughters of the Old Man of the Sea, like the Naiads, they lived in the far side of a dark and underground ocean, towards the Hesperides of the far West, and not far from the site of the Gorgons. Neither Sun nor Moon shine in this dark sea which leads to the realm of Night, where the heavenly bodies disappear into, and re-emanate from, a land under the horizon. In a sense it is all that is unconscious. All that is in *potentia*, not manifest; held in a cosmic womb. A land of pre-birth and after-death.

The Graiae live on a landfall that is called the Land of Rock-roses, a land of pathless forest and rock. In these ancient lands it is probable that even Pallas Athene did not know her way, and it was needful for Perseus to discover the way to the Gorgons from the old gods.

In common with most of the other very ancient female figures they are generally described in an ugly and grotesque form. This is not necessarily the case, though the fact that they were called the 'grey ones' and shared a single eye and a single tooth does conjure an image of grotesque senility. However, greyness does not necessarily mean physical age. Ancient these goddesses certainly are, but, as with other of the 'old and lordly ones' it is possible to be ever young. Their greyness might also be conceived in terms of shimmering morning mist, under moonlight or starlight. And their single eye and single tooth organs of perception of a unique and rare character. The All-Seeing Eye associated with the omniscience of God-head; and the tooth being the three-fold adamantine emblem of the immortal spirit (as in the Qabalah—where the letter Shin means the spirit and a tooth—the hardest organic part of the physical body).

By his having attained the freedom of the inner sea and sky ways as a result of his approach to the cave of the nymphs, the hero Perseus is enabled to approach this other aspect of the three-fold Goddess. This is to attain the spiritual power of omniscient wisdom, the possession of which enables him to penetrate yet deeper into the heart of the Mysteries of manifest existence, to the home of the Gorgons. It is a deep Mystery that he attains this wisdom at the change of the tides, when, in the imagery of the story, the Eye is being passed from one sister to another.

Perseus then proceeds to the very Hesperides themselves, armed with a shield-mirror and a reaping-hook shaped sword. These were both divine gifts, the shield from Pallas Athene, the sword from Hermes. It is these weapons of higher wisdom, which enable him to look upon the Medusa undazzled and to cut off her head in a strange reaping action, just as the heads of the corn are reaped by the sickle. This ancient moon-shaped implement is similar to that used in the earliest Titanic days when Kronos used one to castrate his father Ouranos. That is, it is a cosmic weapon, whose action in one mode created time, and separated the world of space and time from the eternal heavens.

It is now used as a weapon of freedom and redemption in connection with the powers of the Mother—in their crudest and deepest sense.

Something should be said about the origin and nature of the Gorgons, and in particular of Medusa, who was said to be the only mortal one of the three. The two immortal ones were Sthenno (strength) and Euryale (the wide sea), and it is to be noted that they were also ageless. Their collective name (gorgo) is used as a name for little girls so at root they cannot be identified with the ugly and terrible. Medusa has been described as the beautiful cheeked one, and one story relating to her apparent ugliness is that Pallas Athene wrought this affliction upon her as a punishment for making love in the Temple of Wisdom.

Other descriptions of her depict, if not an image of conventional prettiness, a strange and awesome beauty, with golden wings, hands that shine like burnished brass, with boars tusks and with head and body girdled with serpents.

These latter attributes depict the powers of the Gorgons. The boar is a creature of the wild woods traditionally sacred to the goddess. Ancient Celtic heroes went on a boar hunt to the underworld. The sacrifice of pigs was a feature of the ancient rites of Demeter, the Earth Mother, at Eleusis, and the only surviving line of Aeschylus' tragedy, *The Phorkides*, which treats of these ancient Titanic Mysteries is, 'Boar like he passed into the cave'.

The serpents are universal symbols for the creative powers of the feminine. In esoteric psychology and physiology they represent the kundalini—the serpent power. This is not only a phenomenon of the human organism but has its planetary correspondence in the inner forces of the planet. In one aspect it is the reality behind the force fields of ancient sites and trackways, and in a more raw elemental way in the mighty forces of wind, sea, volcano and earthquake. It also represents the generative powers of life. 'The force that through the green fuse drives the flower' in the words of Dylan Thomas. It is essentially a feminine force, and thus is not easily comprehended or come to terms with by the masculine dominated intellect. Hence in the paternally oriented Jewish tradition the serpent appears in the Garden of Eden as a bringer of evil, or at least of temptation.

Whether or not there was a Fall, the serpent power was not the cause of it. There may have been temptation to misuse it, born of the misuse of the freedom of the spiritual will, but the power of physical generation, and its subtle equivalent on inner levels, is not an evil in itself. One might as well say that 'money is the root of all evil'. Certainly money also may be a temptation to the morally weak but it is not evil in itself. Like all manifestations of raw power it simply gives the opportunity for the expression of human motive. It is not evil in itself.

All the old sea powers of the Titanic mythology relate to this power of the feminine, for in ancient times it was predominant in the development of infant man. It is still as much a power today although during the epoch of mankind's adolescence— which covers the historical period—there has been a reversion from the feminine. This may have been a necessary phase but the feminine principle is not something that will simply go away. It pertains as much to God as does the masculine principle. Only in the balanced union of the two can progress to maturity be made. This does not mean a cancelling out of sexual characteristics but a coming to terms with the forces of physically polarized sexuality in balanced expression.

The fact that the developing human consciousness found it necessary to break free from infantile reliance on the Great Mother in order to express its individual Apollonian freedom is what is behind the stories of the wars of the gods. When, for instance in the Greek mythology, Zeus (a male chauvinist, if ever there was one) and the other Olympian deities, replaced the ancient Titans.

Most of these ancient Titans were born of the sea, and their hideous form is but a distortion of their original beauty. The evil and ugliness is in the eye of the beholder. The time has come when these old forces should be recognized for what they are, and redeemed from their neglected, despised and feared position. In this direction lies health and wholeness for the human psyche and its planetary expression. The apparent ugliness should be transformed to its real beauty, for the fearful appearance has been an act of mercy. These great ancient feminine forces appeared as monsters only because mankind could not stand their overwhelming beauty.

This is resumed in the tradition of the messenger of the Holy

Grail, who appears alternately as a fair damsel or a loathly hag. Hero knights such as Gawain married such feminine figures, who were under some kind of enchantment wherein they had to be ugly for at least part of the time. Their restoration to permanent beauty depended on the attitude of the questing knight who courted them. To the pure all things are pure—to the ugly all things are ugly. Blake's 'vegetable glass' reflects to us our true condition, and the mirror is essentially a device of the feminine, reflective principle. It is a tool of ruthlessly honest self-revelation, not of vanity.

It is a valuable exercise therefore to re-evaluate all the ancient powers of primeval mythology, particularly those associated with the sea and night. For these are the forces of the primal creation, the Ain Soph or Limitless sea over which the Holy Spirit breathed the first eddies of manifest form, transforming it into Ain Soph Aur—the Limitless Light of form expression.

Of these are included sisterhoods, (usually three-fold) such as the Fates, the Harpies, the Furies, the Sirens, as well as the Naiads, the Graiae and the Gorgons. Many of them have semi-serpent forms; sometimes figured as fish tails like mermaids or mermen, or otherwise like dragons.

The Pelasgian creation myth is of particular interest. The Pelasgians were an early Greek people who claimed that they originally sprang from dragons' or serpents' teeth—and of no ordinary serpent or dragon either, but of the primal Ophion. Robert Graves suggests that they may have been the neolithic 'Painted Ware' people of c. 3500 BC.

According to mythology the first ever divine being was a goddess, named Eurynome, a kind of primal Aphrodite who arose naked out of the sea of nothingness. In her solitude she danced towards the South thus causing a North wind to blow from the motion of her body. She seized the North wind between her hands and it took on the form of a great serpent, Ophion, who grew enamoured by her dancing and coupled with her. From the union, Eurynome, taking on the form of a dove, laid an egg around which Ophion coiled himself seven times. This hatched out to give birth to all that exists within the universe. Subsequently, according to Robert Graves' reconstruction (in *Greek Myths*), Eurynome bruised the head of Ophion with her heel, and evicted him from their abode on

Mount Olympus to dwell in the caves below the Earth, because
he presumed to claim that it was he who had been creator of all.
From his scattered teeth sprang the first man, and Eurynome
created dual Titanic powers, male and female, to rule over the
seven planetary forces.

Thus, according to this legend Eurynome and Ophion were
the equivalent to the Old Ones of the Sea who ruled over the
Titans before Kronos and Rhea seized power from Ouranos and
Gaia. In later myth, Eurynome still appears, though relegated to
a consort of Zeus to whom she bore the three Charites, from
which our word *charisma* derives, from a root meaning 'to
rejoice'. They are more familiarly known as three Graces, and
are, in a sense, the opposite to the Erinyes, or Furies, the
three-fold agents of retribution.

According to Kerenyi, reporting Pausanias Periegeta, 'a
goddess named Eurynome had a temple in Arcadia, in a spot
difficult of access. This temple was open only once a year. The
cult-image of her showed a woman with a fish's tail and in
golden chains. The inhabitants of the region supposed her to be
Artemis, but better educated people remembered that, according to Homer and Hesiod, Eurynome was a daughter of
Oceanos, and that she and Thetis received Hephaistos in their
lap, in the depths of the waters, when he was flung into the sea.'

This imagery is important, providing ancient links between
the heavenly and the underworld powers. Hephaistos, the great
smith of the gods, often depicted as a lame dwarf, was the
misbegotten child of Hera, the queen of the Olympian gods,
who threw him from heaven into the sea, to be saved and
nurtured by the ancient goddesses Thetis and Eurynome, for
whom he fashioned jewellery in a grotto by the great
underground sea. He also had as his companion the Kabeiroi,
another line of ancient underworld gods and servants of the
Great Mother—who were sea-gods and smiths. And later he
became associated with the volcanic powers of Etna and
Vesuvius.

His importance in ancient myth is preserved in confused and
conflicting stories about births engendered by Zeus and Hera. It
is said that Hera bore Hephaistos unaided as an act of spite and
emulation when Zeus bore Pallas Athene from his head.
Another story says that Hephaistos assisted in the birth of Pallas

Athene by cleaving Zeus' head with an axe. Then there is the tradition that Hera bore a dragon, Typhaon, in revenge for Pallas Athene, whom she gave to the dragoness Delphine, who in ancient times operated the oracle at Delphi before it was taken over by Apollo. She was also depicted as half woman half serpent. A variation of the story records the mother of Typhaon to have been Gaia, the most ancient goddess of the Earth, at the behest of Hera.

Giving birth to a dragon seems more characteristic of the attributes of Gaia than of Hera, although the latter might well have provided the motivation. Gaia, according to the cosmology of Hesiod, gave birth to the Titans, as well as the mountains and seas, along with many other forms of Earth life, in union with the great sky factor Ouranos. Hera was thus invoking a great ancient dragon form of the primal generative powers of earth. This is described evocatively by Kerenyi: (*The Gods of the Greeks* p. 152):

> Thereupon Hera went apart also from the other gods. She prayed and smote the earth with her palm: 'Hear me, Gaia and Ouranos, thou who art on high, and you Titans who dwell beneath the earth in Tartaros, you who are the ancestors of gods and men: hear me, all of you, and give me a son who shall not be weaker than Zeus himself! As Zeus was mightier than Kronos, so let my son be mightier than he!' She struck the earth with powerful hand, Gaia, the source of life, quivered; and Hera rejoiced, for she guessed that she had her will.

The power of the ancient gods may be seen in that even the Queen of the Olympians has to invoke them for aid. Also, the connection with the great oracular centre of Delphi, is significant. This was a centre of focus for the ancient feminine powers, for it was Delphine who reigned supreme there, and the later serpent/dragon Typhaon, or Python, who was put in her charge. His lair was in a cave by a spring—a location that is the hallmark of any source of psychic power. Another version has him coiled about a tree—an equally indicative symbolic location. Furthermore, in this case it was a laurel tree, giving an Apollonian connection.

The name Delphine, from which Delphi derives, is connected according to Kerenyi, with an old word meaning 'womb'. The oracular priestesses of Delphi were termed Pythonesses, after Delphine's consort Python.

The cause of the later connection of Apollo with Delphi is somewhat confused in the myths. We are dealing with fragments of very ancient oral tradition that are like pieces of patchwork that have to be assembled into a coherent fabric. Some versions depict this as a violent acquisition, others imply that the violence was an error later to be atoned for, whilst there are other pictures depicting Apollo and Python in accord, mutually guarding the omphalos stone—the sacred stone considered to be the centre of the universe.

Much would seem to depend on the changing character of Apollo—or rather how mankind related to his archetype—for all such relationships are in a process of change with the gradual evolution of consciousness. Solar heroes in particular tend to transform in this way. The character of Gawain in the Arthuriad is a particularly clear example. In the aspect of the 'enlightenment' of intellect the Apollonian powers can be equated with much that is at variance with the old dark feminine powers of the earth. However, the conflict is one that should be a polar creative tension rather than a rending source of disaster. The Apollonian powers are the natural urge for growth to individualization. Thus we see a temporary, or temporal, conflict of role but one that is evil only in the over-reaction or unbalance of man. In the individual this can be painful, as with all problems of adolescence, but they are for the most part outgrown without permanent damage. When a whole race is undergoing the adolescent phase then obviously the risks and dangers are more far reaching. This is the root of the current concern for a proper regard for the feminine. It is the way to responsible racial social maturity.

Indeed, the proper balance is clearly shown in the fact that Apollo is the twin brother of the moon goddess Artemis. They were both children of Leto, the ever mild and gracious granddaughter of Ouranos and Gaia, whose father had been the Titan Koios, whose name, Kerenyi records, means the sphere of the heavens, and who was also called Polos, referring to the celestial polar axis. Leto's mother was Phoibe, a goddess of the moon, whose name meant purifying one. It is from her that Apollo was later sometimes to be called Phoebus Apollo.

It is said that Leto wandered through many countries seeking a place to give birth to her children—in common with other goddesses who wandered for various reasons: Demeter, Isis, Io, and others. Appropriately the time of birth of the twins was to be dusk, the time of balance between night and day. This time is called 'wolf light', and there are also traditions that she was protected by wolves during this time, or even that she temporarily turned into a wolf herself.

Other traditions should be mentioned that show evidence of the connection between ancient sea, feminine, stellar and underworld powers. Leto had a sister Asteria, which means Star goddess, and who was the mother of another moon goddess, Hecate, closely related to Artemis. After Zeus had fathered Apollo and Artemis on Leto he had pursued her sister Asteria, who escaped him by turning into a stone and falling into the depths of the sea. She emerged as an island on which Leto could give birth to her twins. This is usually identified with Delos which also had the tradition of having once been a floating island, an ocean wanderer hidden from the eyes of men. At the birth of Apollo and Artemis it became firmly anchored to the sea bed with four great pillars, and is described evocatively, as quoted by Kerenyi, as a 'widely visible star of the dark earth'.

There is a certain alchemical element about the descriptions of rejoicing when Leto eventually gave birth on Delos. All the gods rejoiced, the former rocky and barren outcrop became fruitful, singing swans circled the island becoming mute after the seventh time, nymphs sang a sacred birthing song, the foundations of the island turned to gold, as did the waters of its river and circular lake, and also the leaves of the olive trees.

All of this brings us back to the traditions surrounding Perseus, whose mother Danäe was also associated with heavenly gold. We left him approaching the Gorgon Medusa, with mirror-shield and crescent-sword; higher moon powers, in a sense, given by Pallas Athene. By coming to terms with the higher principles of the feminine wisdom, the old devouring mother who sucks her immature children back into the womb, in a living death, can be overcome by the individualized hero. In a very physical symbolic sense, the sack in which the head of the Medusa is contained could be described as the sac of the testes, the scrotum, the filling of which with the creative seed is the prerequisite of man-hood.

The Medusa head is later incorporated in the armour of
Pallas Athene. This may also be understood to indicate that
without the Medusa powers, the higher wisdom is a mere
attenuated idealism lacking human substance, and inadequately
related to the realities of life experience. A weedy growth of a
seed with insufficient root, and not at all uncommon in idealistic
esoteric circles.

It is on his way back from the Gorgon's lair that Perseus
appropriately meets the woman who is to become his wife. This
is Andromeda, chained to a rock, the impending victim of a
marauding sea-monster. With the powers that he now has from
confronting and overcoming the Medusa he is able to release
her. These powers are those of a spiritual and psychological
coming to maturity.

When the Medusa was slain by Perseus it is said that two
creatures were born. Some say this was from drops of her blood
falling into the sea—others that she was pregnant by Poseidon
the sea god and carried them already in her womb. Either
version is adequate to the inner meaning. The blood is the
vehicle of expression of the spirit; the sea is the universal
creative matrix. Their intermingling is similar to a conception by
the god of the sea. In either case the two creatures are the
powers represented by the Medusa raised to a higher
expression. They are Pegasus, the winged horse, and Chrysaor,
a hero with a golden sword.

Pegasus is usually considered to be the emblem of poetic
inspiration. He is however more than this. The winged horse is
an archetype of the type of priest who not merely acts as a
channel for divine force but can carry others to great spiritual
heights and far inner realms. He is therefore an archetype of the
magician-priest—which is of course similar to that of a poet or
dramaturge in the highest sense; a bard, or story-teller, a
conductor of 'path workings'.

Perseus, by confronting the three-fold triple goddesses, has
released mighty creative powers on many levels of being, besides
being able to rescue and mate with the heroine Andromeda.

Andromeda is chained by reason of the folly of her mother,
Cassiopeia, who, in an act of overweening pride, claimed that
her beauty was greater than that of the sea nymphs. As a
consequence the kingdom was flooded by an uprush of the sea

and was also ravaged by a fearsome sea monster, Cetus.

There is in this a parallel with the story of Noah's flood, or the Atlantean deluge. Once again overweening pride brings retribution, as it must, for it is an unbalancing of the natural order.

The vanity of the mother must also imply the denigration of the daughter as well as all other expressions of the feminine such as the sea nymphs, hence her being chained to a rock to be ravished or slain by the monster from the depths. It is also a mirror image of the condition of immaturity represented by Perseus before he has conquered the Great Terrible Mother as Medusa. Now that he has achieved his quest not only are the higher powers of the Medusa released, as her progeny, but he can release the feminine principle as mate, rather than mother, and so, as in the Quest of the Holy Grail, release the land from enchantment or inundation by uncontrollable forces. Andromeda helps Perseus to overcome the sea monster by passing stones to him. This is not without significance. There is a down-to-earth quality in the feminine contact in the role of mate.

Perseus overcomes the monster finally by the powers of the Medusa head. The serpent powers are now his. Following from this he overcomes the male rivals for the hand of his bride, and goes on to rescue his mother Danäe and Diktys the Fisher King. The Gorgon head is dedicated to Pallas Athene who has worn it on her shield and breast armour ever since. The other gifts which had enabled him to journey to the interior, over the underworld sea, are returned to the nymphs, and Perseus returns with his mother and wife to Argos.

The whole of the Perseus mythology is of relevance to the Goddess powers, and our consideration of them will not be complete until we have examined their central holy of holies, the Garden of the Hesperides. This was in the far West of the great underground sea of Okeanos. It was sometimes said to lie at the far end of a red sea. This is another allusion to the far West, and the apparent path to it is made by the setting sun inflaming the waters with its reflection.

In later Olympean mythologies it was said that Zeus, the king of the gods, had a palace there. This emphasizes their importance, but their origin is more accurately indicated in the belief that they were the possession of Hera, the Queen of the gods, and had been given to her as a wedding gift by Gaia, the most ancient Earth goddess, the source of all life on earth. The marriage bed of Hera was even said to be located here, and the creative aspect was emphasized by the fruitfulness of the earth and by the many fountains that jetted forth. It was the site also of an orchard and in particular of a special tree which bore golden apples. This tree was guarded by a serpent, called Ladon, which is also the name of a river in Arcadia. This is not inappropriate, for Arcadia was by tradition an idyllic pastoral land, and a river is one of the most ancient symbols for the fount of life. One of the ancient Greek creation myths saw all life as having come from a primal river, Eridanus, which also has a constellation dedicated to it, that stretches along the horizon between the celestial hemispheres.

Ladon was variously considered to be either the son or the brother of a primeval serpent goddess called Echidna, who was both male and female in disposition, but in appearance was a young woman of great beauty from the waist up, and of serpentine form from the waist down. As Kerenyi remarks, in *The Gods of the Greeks*:

> In the stories, as told in our oldest mythology, of any god or goddess of the great family of Phorkys, Proteus and Neseus (i.e., of the ancient sea gods G.K.)—or of the corresponding old gods of the earth, such as Typhon or the Athenian Kekrops or the Kychreus of Salamis—it is always difficult to make out whether the deity concerned was believed to resemble, in the parts below the hips, a serpent, a dolphin or a fish.

The dolphin, it should be added, is a sea creature with a womb. Echidna was, according to Hesiod, immortal and ageless; and she gave birth to many of the creatures associated with the tests of initiation and the boundary between the worlds of life and death. These included Kerberos, the three-headed hound who guarded the entrance to Hades; and Orthos, a two-headed hound with a serpent's tail—or alternatively with seven serpent heads. Orthos became the hound of Geryoneus, the strongest man in the world, who was the three-headed son of Chrysaor, the hero of the golden sword who had sprung from the womb of Medusa along with Pegasus. Orthos helped guard the red cattle of Geryon, which were the envy of the world, and kept by Geryon in his kingdom of the West. They were identified by some as the red clouds of the evening sky.

Orthos and Echidna between them also begot the Sphinx, which appears in the saga of the hero Oedipus—another who had to contend with the forces of the Mother.

Another of Echidna's children was the Chimaira, a composite lion, goat and serpent overcome by the hero Bellerophon. And it would be right, according to some authorities, to include Ladon in the progeny of this primordial nymph. However his especial key position, guarding the golden apples of the Hesperides, suggests that it might be more fitting to regard him as the brother of Echidna—both being progeny of Gaia and Typhaon—Earth Form and Serpent Power. Like Echidna, Ladon had his dwelling in underground caves beneath the golden apple trees of the West.

He was assisted in his task by the Hesperides. The Hesperides, usually four in number, were beautiful young women as their names imply. Kerenyi gives a selection from various sources, which include: Hesperia—the one of the evening; Aigle—the luminous one; Erytheia—the crimson one; Arethousa, who is a goddess of springs; Lipara—soft radiance; Chrysothemis—golden law and order; Asterope—star brilliant; and even Medousa. They are associated with a number of other female beings, the serpent nymphs, who frequent the Garden of the Hesperides. The double flute is an instrument associated with them, the tones of which, at dusk, called the initiated to their rites. They were particularly associated with the magic of harmonic sound by virtue of their bright song, and Ladon himself had the gift of many voices. So beautiful was their singing that they have been associated with the Sirens. They had a similar birth to Pegasus and Chrysaor in that they sprang from the blood of one of the great creatures of ancient time when overcome by a hero—in this case when Heracles overcame the great originating river god in the form of a bull-headed serpent. This primeval creativity became transformed into those capable of ravishingly beautiful song, so beautiful that sailors feared them, for to hear their song was to be entranced by them forever. As a result of these seamens' tales they have been depicted in monstrous guise but in fact were originally fair creatures whose name associates them with the humming of bees.

In other legends they are held to be companions of Persephone, the Queen of the Underworld (and in this role, daughter of Clithon, the depths of the earth). Their enticing travellers into the realms of the Underworld is in this respect an alleviation of the pangs of death and indeed hides ancient rites for the safe and proper conduct of the soul at the dissolution of the body—an art which seems retained only in the ritual of *The Tibetan Book of the Dead*, but which once had a more universal practice as other Books of the Dead testify. A Book of the Dead is also, of course, closely parallel to a manual of initiation, which is an introduction to the inner realms without the soul completely severing from the body.

The Sirens were also sometimes depicted as birds who carried human souls, or at very least their prayers, to heaven. It is the attempt at pictorial representation of their various attributes that renders most of these ancient deities into monstrous form, bird-headed women with sphinx like claws for instance; and their association with the realm of the dead, or the Underworld, likewise exacerbated the fears of the ignorant and the superstitious into regarding them as nightmare figures.

Similar fate, in the literature, attended the swan-like maidens known as the Graiae, whom we have already mentioned, and also the Harpies, who were sisters of Iris, the rainbow. They were associated with the wind, and their names variously mean swift-footed or swift of flight. They could carry souls off to the inner realms, hence their rather frightening title of 'snatchers'; however, they are also associated with swift footed horses and so have much in common with the heavenly inspirer, Pegasus. The rushing wind is also a universal title for the Spirit, or the Holy Spirit, the wind that bloweth where it listeth.

Probably the most fearsome of all these children of the ancient sea mythology are the three Furies, the Erinyes, or Eumenides, who, like Medusa, had snakes in place of hair. However, they are but agents of karma, or divine justice, and transformed when justice had been done. When they first pursued Orestes for having killed his mother they were black but when, in one version of the story, he chewed his finger off in remorse they turned to white. In the region associated with the Orestian tragedy they were given sacrifices and divine honour in conjunction with the Charites or Graces, of whom they are the counterpart, for another name for them is the Benevolent, which shows they were not mere personifications of anger and revenge.

They were variously held to be daughters of the sea, the earth or the underworld. Ouranos, and Gaia, Phorkys and Eurynome, Hades and Persephone, amongst others, are cited as their parents, and all are appropriate in one aspect or another.

Their function, and relevance to a matriarchal age, is expounded clearly by Kerenyi '. . . above all they represented the Scolding Mother. Whether a mother was insulted, or perhaps even murdered, the Erinyes apeared. Like swift bitches they pursued all who had flouted blood-kinship and the deference due to it. They defended the rights of the father, and also of the elder brother; but especially they supported the claims of the mother, even when these were unjust.' At the close of Aeschylus' Oresteian trilogy they are redeemed and placated by Pallas Athene, mediating between them and Apollo.

We may conclude our examination of these ancient goddess forms by reference to the Morai, or Fates. They have a particular relevance to the dynamics of the magic circle of birth and death. Their number varied from two to four; although they are more generally recognized as a trinity. When only two are considered, as at Delphi, they are regarded respectively as guardians of the gates of birth and of death.

In their triune form Klotho is the spinner of the thread of life; Lachesis measures the length that the thread is to be; and Atropos cuts it with her shears, bringing about physical death. They lived in a cave, in the inner worlds, from whence white water gushes—in one sense the waters of life, in another sense (and closely associated with it in its inner dynamics) moonlight.

They can also be regarded as aspects of a simple primeval goddess, sitting at the centre of the circle, spinning the web of life in the worlds of form.

The Labours of Heracles
We have emphasized that myths of the hero represent a stage in the evolution of consciousness, when the individuality is being asserted to break free from the aura of the mother. The myth of Heracles is particularly indicative of this stage, for most of his

feats involve a fight against the old maternal forces represented by the ancient serpent or dragon monsters.

Even the birth of Heracles foreshadows his intended archetypal pattern or destiny. He is fathered by Zeus, that most masculine of gods (except perhaps for the Jewish Jehovah), with the express intention of his being a hero of gods and of men. His mother is Alcmene, the wife of the King Amphitryon (a grandson of Perseus) who is away at the wars; and according to Hesiod she is chosen because she was 'incorruptible'. Also of note is a certain familiar three-fold aspect in his conception, in that Zeus made one night as long as three. There is a parallel to the conception of King Arthur in that Zeus appeared to Alcmene and lay with her in the guise of her husband. Finally the especial nature is marked by the fact that Zeus, at her death, reserved a place for Alcmene in the Hesperides.

Not unnaturally Hera, the queen of the gods, is averse to Heracles, although not simply as a consequence of his being the progeny of yet another of Zeus' infidelities. There is an important weaning element here, the story being that Zeus lay the infant Heracles at her breast when she was asleep; when she awoke and pushed him away the milk from her breast sprayed across the heavens to form the Milky Way. This incident was contrived by Zeus in order to make Heracles immortal. It contains two significant truths—one that the whole galactic system stems from the feminine principle; secondly that it is from this principle that humanity spiritually springs; and that both it and humankind are of the quality of eternal spirit.

In the cradle Heracles commences his destiny of gaining freedom from the ancient mother forces by killing with his bare hands two serpents that were sent by Hera to kill him. The image of a priestess holding a serpent in each hand is a powerful one that indicates the old divine feminine power. It is seen in certain old Minoan ware but stems traditionally from Atlantis. The image of the infant Heracles in the similar posture but strangling the serpents indicates his mission.

He subsequently grows to manhood. His traditional muscle-bound aspect may be indicative of the narcissific motivation of male adolescence although this in fact is a later Roman convention.

He is soon embroiled in many adventures, and in common

with other greater archetypal figures, he has tended over the centuries to absorb adventures not originally his own. However, those which involve the struggle against the maternal feminine are plainly his, and in particular the famous Twelve Labours of Heracles.

The reason for the imposition of these was originally the instigation of Hera, who inflicted him with madness. Seeing his children as enemies he began to shoot them down with his bow and arrow. This is a strange inversion of the function of Eros, the son of Venus, but represents a stage in adolescence of revolt against the responsibilities of family. To the immature male this seems like an unbearable domination engineered by the feminine; the mother reasserting herself in a new guise. It is not inappropriate for the war-lording of the whole historical period which has covered the adolescent phase of the human group soul.

On recovering his sanity Heracles tries to atone for his guilt by blocking off all communication, confining himself in a dark underground cell, but this living death of remorse is not the way through; he is induced to seek advice from the old oracular shrine of the Goddess at Delphi, which binds him to the quest of the Twelve Labours.

We will list these with a brief indication of their import, but there is no substitute for long and deep study and meditation upon the myths themselves.

1. *The Nemean Lion.* In one tradition this was the creature of Selene the goddess of the moon, and lived in a deep underground cave with two openings. It was let loose upon the Nemean people when they refused to sacrifice to the goddess. It was, however, also regarded as born of the serpent goddess Echidna, sired by the two-headed serpent hound Orthos, and therefore a brother of the Sphinx, which means that it had the function of guarding the threshold of Mysteries of Initiation. In the Theban cycle, Oedipus had to answer the Sphinx's questions before proceeding further, a familiar type of challenge at the door of initiation.

No weapon could prevail against this lion and it was necessary that Heracles wrestle with it and overcome it by his own unaided strength and skill. The demands of this task caused him to fall into a deep sleep, which almost cost him the fruits of victory, but sleep is a lesser form of death, and again affirms the initiatory aspect of this first labour. When he awoke Heracles made for himself a crown of wild celery, a plant associated in those times with the wreaths placed on tombs.

Thus the conquering of the sphinx/lion of Nemea is an opening phase in an initiation sequence, indicating that the test in hand is the overcoming of the forces of death and rebirth, and the assertion of the individual immortality of the human spirit. Heracles became associated with the hide of the lion, for he flayed the beast after he had killed it, with one of its claws (the Claw of the Lion is a symbol familiar to freemasonry), and wore it ever afterward as a sign of his mission.

There are astrological connections with this opening labour in that it is associated also with the first sign of the Zodiac, the Ram. A ram was sacrificed in celebration of the overcoming of the lion by a representative of primeval man whose son had been killed by the lion, which was itself translated into another Fire sign of the Zodiac, as the constellation Leo.

2. *The Hydra of Lerna.* This was another of the old serpent powers—the child of the serpentine god forms Typhon and Echidne. It lived in an area renowned for very deep underground springs, associated with the ancient nymphs, and was guardian of this entrance to the Underworld. This was the gate associated with the Dionysos cycle. The Hydra was commonly regarded as sister of Kerberos, the three-headed dog that guards Hades beyond the River Styx. She lived among the water logged roots of a huge plane tree.

The opening phase in Heracles' struggle against the Hydra was the shooting of flaming arrows into her lair. We may regard the fire as emblematic of the human spirit, in the same tradition that regarded fire as the expression of the divine spark that the Titan hero Prometheus brought to humanity within a hollow wand (the spinal column) from heaven. The bow and arrow are associated with Cupid and represent the powers of love, which is, or should be, the unique contribution of the expressed human spirit to the created world. Cupid is the son of Venus/Aphrodite the goddess of love; and at a further stage back in the history of mythology, the worlds were begun by the primeval Eros, a huge awesome figure of universal love, or the desire of God.

Heracles is not invincible and alone in this struggle. He needs the help of a lesser mortal, his nephew Iolas, who again uses the power of fire, the expression of the individual human spirit, to seal the severed necks of the many-headed Hydra, after Heracles has cut off the heads. Otherwise they would grow again. This is indicative of ultimate individual spiritual responsibility of all human souls. We cannot be dragged into heaven on a sledge, entirely vicariously. Even the most vicariously oriented theology demands at least 'belief', which is a mode of expression of correctly oriented free will.

A whole forest was used up in the provision of flaming spiritual brands, an oblique symbolic reference to the uprooting of the dark forest that is widely used as representation of the condition of the material world. The heroes are also beset by crabs which come to the aid of the Hydra. Crabs are one form used to represent certain sea nymphs and emphasize the origin of the Hydra's powers in the great maternal primeval sea. The sign of the Crab figures in the Zodiac also, and as it is the first sign of the subterranean celestial hemisphere it is sometimes called the Gate of Descending Souls. It is also, appropriately, a water sign. Hydra is also represented in the heavens by a very long constellation whose head commences at Cancer and proceeds round the Zodiacal belt as far as Libra the Scales. Thus release for descending souls may be seen as a matter of achieving cosmic balance.

3. *The Erymanthean Boar.* The boar hunt is an ancient underworld venture, and the creature is sacred to the goddess, in this instance particularly in her aspect as Artemis. It had to be taken alive. This labour is particularly associated with centaurs. It thus has astrological representation in the constellation Centaurus, which lies low on the horizon and in fact is never seen completely from the Northern hemisphere. It contains the very bright Alpha Centauri, the nearest of the bright stars to our Earth. The Zodiacal sign Sagittarius is also often depicted in centaur form.

The great centaur Chiron was associated with the hero Jason as well as with Heracles. There are deep mysteries connected with him and he may be equated with the human condition that expresses higher intelligence in animal form. However, there are risks in this condition for the intelligence can still be expressed in contending forms. This is represented in the Heracles legend by a great battle of the centaurs, which in fact starts as a result of Heracles opening up the wine store of the centaurs—a gift from Dionysos but one that the centaurs did not understand and found difficult to handle. It may be taken to mean the intoxication that can result from direct spiritual awareness.

In this battle, which may be assumed to be the historical human condition, the most wise and righteous of the centaurs, Chiron, is wounded by one of Heracles' arrows. These now had been dipped in the Hydra's blood, which meant that there was no cure for anyone scratched by them. Chiron undergoes prolonged suffering, for he can neither live fully nor die; a condition portraying the immortal human spirit bound to the wheel of life and death. Eventually Chiron's suffering is ended when he is allowed to take the place of Prometheus, who can in turn be released from his bondage as a consequence. In other words, the centaur is a transitional human condition, that passes when the Promethean given spirit is fully expressed in divine man—an achievement which fully justifies and releases Prometheus.

The centaur Pholos is also killed by one of Heracles' Hydra-envenomed arrows, and Heracles buries him before passing on to hunt the boar. This is an indication that a phase in human growth and redemption is reached in this labour—that of the passing of the half animal man.

The boar is significantly captured by Heracles driving it upwards, towards higher consciousness, until, driven beyond its natural limits, it falls unconscious above the snow line, and can be caught in Heracles' snare.

4. *The Hind of Cerynis.* This was a creature belonging to Artemis the moon goddess. Four others pulled her chariot. This again had to be taken alive and not harmed. It was then returned to the goddess. It was of particular significance because of its antlers—not normal on a hind—and also because they were golden. The hunted horned beast figures in many legend cycles

and its particular danger to the hunter is that it leads him on and on into strange lands and states of being from which he is very lucky to return. Indeed one tradition has it that the natural home of the hind, and to which it lures its would-be captors, is beneath the trees of golden apples guarded by the serpent Ladon, in the Garden of the Hesperides at the world's end.

Heracles followed it for the cycle of a whole year and through many lands not generally known to ordinary mortals, and as one consequence of these travels brought back, as well as the captured hind, the wild olive—the tree sacred to Pallas Athene and also representing, like her, the higher wisdom.

5. *The Stymphalian Birds.* These infested woods and fields in Arcadia. Heracles had to find some method of controlling them and was aided by the wisdom of Pallas Athene, who assisted many heroes, including Perseus. She represents the higher feminine principle, the intuition, which man needs to develop. With her inspiration Heracles fashioned a bronze rattle, which must have a parallel with the instrument sacred to Isis, the sistrum.

The Stymphalian Birds have much in common with the bird-like ancient feminine forces, such as the Harpies and Sirens. They may also be regarded however as the shades of the restless dead, wandering in the underworld and even in the overworld, confused, noisy, squabbling, unoriented except for the instinctual mass movements of the herd or flock. Heracles brings the knowledge of the higher wisdom to them by the musical instrument of the goddess that over-rides their clatter. He also shoots a number with his arrows of love.

6. *The Augean Stables* had to be cleaned in a day. King Augeus never needed to clean them because his livestock was so perfect as to be immune from disease. His kingdom was not of this world, for the sun shone from his eyes and his name means radiance; indeed his kingdom in the West was in fact an outer part of the Hesperides. It would appear to have represented an intermediate state between inner and outer planes and that this was to the detriment of the latter. The dung from the inner stables caused corruption and disease on the outer levels. Heracles overcame this form of psychic congestion by diverting

the flow of a river—a superb demonstration of control of the creative force in a constructive manner.

A story associated with this labour depicts a similar kind of condition, but under different symbolism, wherein Heracles kills a centaur who has forced himself upon a human girl as her bridegroom. Again the principle is one of finding a means to end an ill-assorted conjunction.

7. *The Cretan Bull* represented ancient force running wild, trampling vineyards and fields and some authorities identify it with the one sent by Poseidon, the god of the sea, from which sprang the minotaur as a result of Queen Pasiphae's unnatural lust. Heracles controlled and captured it, and it was later released to play a part in the hero quest of Theseus.

8. *The Horses of Diomedes* ate human flesh until Heracles turned them upon their master after which they became normal and docile. In some pictures of them they are winged, and indeed the horse was associated with death in Greek times, whether pulling a hearse or bearing a dead hero to heaven. A horse looking through a window is indicative of funeral rites. This labour of Heracles is therefore concerned with victory over certain of the forces of death, and the ability to control them rather than to be their victim, figuratively torn to pieces and eaten by them.

9. *The Girdle of Hippolyta* belonged to an Amazon queen, one of a female race who hated men yet emulated masculine characteristics. This is a not unfamiliar syndrome of the immature feminine seeking to express itself. Heracles obtained the girdle by so impressing Hippolyta that she gave it to him. Another version considers that he stole it but this does not ring true and is more an interpolation of the Theseus legend cycle.

10. *The Cattle of Geryon* brings us close to the supreme achievement of the final labours. These cattle belonged to the son of Chrysaor, who sprang with Pegasus from the Medusa. He was three-headed—an allusion to the guardianship of the Underworld and the realms of the three-fold goddess; and also was the strongest man in the world, for what man could

overcome death? The herds of cattle were kept in the far West, towards the Hesperides. Popular tradition associates the herds with the reddened clouds of sunset. Heracles needed divine help for this mission and sailed over the underworld sea in a golden cup given him by Helios the sun god.

A parallel with the Grail Quest springs to mind. The Mystery element within this journey is confirmed by the story that when he reached his destination in the far West Heracles set up two Pillars. Esoterically this signifies the principle of balance between the modes of manifestation of spiritual force. Exoterically they become the Pillars of Heracles at the Straits of Gibraltar, each on a separate continent, and dividing the inner, middle-of-the-world, sea, the Mediterranean, from the great ocean beyond. Once established in the far West Heracles killed the two-headed dog, Orthos (a combination of the guardian dog deity, and of Janus, who looks both ways, to outer and inner). He also killed Geryon and loading the cattle into the golden cup of Helios brought them back to the outer world. The powerful significance of this labour is emphasized in the incident wherein when Hera intervened to assist Geryon. Heracles wounded her in the breast with an arrow. The cup was eventually returned to Helios.

11. *The Apples of the Hesperides.* This penultimate labour takes Heracles so close to the centre of things that it is sometimes cited as the last labour. However, this is esoterically incorrect, for the final labour must be the harrowing of hell and the overcoming of the powers of Death. To approach the garden in the far West where the Tree of Life grows in the form of an apple tree bearing golden fruit is, however, a similar feat of overcoming natural inner boundaries, the one symbolized in the Old Testament by the angel who prevents mankind returning to the Garden of Eden, the Earthly Paradise.

As with Perseus, so did Heracles need to consult the nymphs for advice on how to cross the inner sea, and he obtained the means of going there by wrestling with the shape-shifting Old Man of the Sea to whom they had directed him.

Another version says that he used the cup of Helios once again but there are various ways of attaining the Garden of the Hesperides and an alternative, less direct route is described in the legends that tell how Heracles obtained the help of the great Titans Prometheus and Atlas.

Prometheus was still chained to a rock for his act of bringing divine fire from heaven to aid the human race. An eagle came to devour his liver each day but Heracles shot the bird with his weapon of love, the bow and arrow. This act shows the releasing of the old Titan from the consequences of the sins of the spiritual will, which are elsewhere called the Fall. Heracles now represents justified, redeemed, spiritually mature humanity, and the victory of this spiritual demonstration justifies and releases the higher powers that enabled mankind, as a species, to exist above the animals and below the angels.

Prometheus refers Heracles to Atlas, the Titan who carries not only the Earth upon his back but also the axle upon which the heavens revolve. The two are of course intimately connected in that the circuit of the heavens is an appearance resulting from the axial movement of the Earth. It is Prometheus' advice that Heracles should not attempt to seize the fruits of Paradise by violence but by request of the aid of the powers that hold the machinery of the universe in balanced motion. Atlas agrees to conform, but while he goes to fetch the golden apples it is needful for Heracles to take his place, holding the balance of the manifest universe. This is similar to the role of an achieved buddha in Mahayana Buddhism who does not go on to unmanifest glories but remains looking back to the world, mediating love and aid to those who have not yet achieved, refusing to go on until all have attained their full potential as realized spiritual beings. In this part of the task Heracles is also aided by the higher wisdom of Pallas Athene.

Other versions say that it was necessary for him to aid Atlas by killing the serpent Ladon, that guarded the Tree, with his bow and arrow. That is, human love as manifested in the spiritually achieved human transcends the old serpent powers. Once the golden apples are achieved the old tale (whereby Atlas attempts to trick Heracles to retain the burden of the earth and sky, and is tricked himself into taking it back) is simply the matter of choice that lies before the spiritually attained human being.

The golden apples, as the fruit of the gods, cannot be retained on Earth, and after they have been shown as evidence of the successful completion of Heracles' task, they are returned by Pallas Athene to the Hesperides.

12. *The Stealing of Cerberus.* This final labour was a journey to the Underworld. This time quite specifically to the land of the dead, and again Heracles needed the assistance of Pallas Athene and Hermes (as did Perseus). First he overcame the initial barrier between the worlds, the river Styx, in forcing Charon the ferryman to take him across, although he was not dead. The close connection between the powers of love and death is shown in the sequence where he is first approached by the shade of Meleagar whose sister he afterwards married. Hermes instructs Heracles that he has nothing to fear from the dead. His real confrontation is with Hades, the Lord of the Underworld, whom he overcomes in direct combat, and then, in turn, the great three-headed guardian dog of the Underworld. Pallas Athene, the goddess of higher wisdom, is needed to row him and his prize back to the land of the living.

Part Three:
The Rosicrucian Transformation Process

It is little realized how far the ancient forces of the Feminine Mysteries are resumed in the Rosicrucian documents of the early seventeenth century. But here, in the form of baroque symbolism, are the same very ancient dynamics: in the detailed tomb symbolism of the *Fama Fraternitatis*; and in the wealth of sacrificial, alchemical and feminine symbolism in the *Chymical Marriage of Christian Rosencreutz*.

These particular documents crystallize a general movement of the group soul of Western Europe at the time. Briefly, the *Fama Fraternitatis*, which is first reported as having been seen in manuscript form in 1610, tells of the foundation of a secret brotherhood by one Christian Rosencreutz, ostensibly a fifteenth-century German of noble lineage, who had, from childhood, been dedicated to the study of the secrets of the universe. To this end he had travelled in the Near and Middle East and finally Morocco, learning the language and sciences of the Arabians, particularly mathematics, medicine and magic. Returning to Europe via Spain he found however that there was no interest in the wisdom he had to impart. The learned of Europe were in no way disposed to come to terms with these 'new axiomata, whereby all things might fully be restored. But it was to them a laughing matter; and being a new thing unto them, they feared that their great name should be lessened, if they should now again begin to learn and acknowledge their many years errors, to which they were accustomed, and wherewith they had gained them enough.'

Then as now, the inner principles of the natural world were

felt to be irrelevant, unnecessary and bothersome to material expediency and established assumptions.

Accordingly, on his return to Germany, Christian Rosencreutz decided to form a sacred college of those who were capable of applying the secrets of mathematics, medicine and magic that he had learned. At first there were just four of them, himself and three others, known by the initials G.Y.; J.A.; and J.O. 'After this manner,' says the *Fama*, 'began the Fraternity of the Rose Cross.' They proceeded to compile a great book of their wisdom in a magical language and writing, and to construct a building called the Sanctis Spiritis. These, it should be understood, are inner rather than outer artefacts, and to be sought by the inner eye and inner ear rather than by the organs of the outer sense. That is the meaning of the saying that the books were written in magical language and the building that of the Holy Spirit. They then extended their membership from four to eight—in the Qabalistic symbolism of numbers from 1 + 3 to 1 + 7. This implies existence on another plane of expression from the original principle. That is, the Founder commenced by appointing a trio to give expression to his ideas, (the three being Qabalistically the basic figure of form), and then proceeded to an organization of seven (the full complement of inner types of force) working with him.

Having established themselves as a centre of inner plane force, they then undertook the next phase of their work, which was of physical dispersal.

This principle of formation and dispersal is fundamental to the growth of the Mystery tradition. It is little understood by students who often wonder why there is not a permanent large organization formed to teach the secret wisdom. This is an unrealistic expectation. Wild flowers spread by distributing their seeds in many ways, not by growing bigger and bigger.

As a unifying principle the brothers agreed upon a rule. This is the cement that holds the true Mystery Tradition together— the inner agreement as to principle, rather than a specific outer organization.

In general terms this rule decreed that:

1. They would each work for the cure of souls, seeking no fee;
2. They would not be distinguishable by any outer form of dress but would conform to the custom of wherever they were;

3.   They would link together on the inner at least once per year;
4.   Each would select and train a successor;
5.   The name Christian Rosencreutz would symbolize their ideals;
6.   The society would remain secret until firmly established i.e., after a century of continued existence.

These represent guidelines that remain valid as the ideals for any inner group. Indeed from this nucleus an inner focus was formed that has provided the growing point and catalyst for all genuinely contacted esoteric groups and individuals in the West. In short, the Fraternity of Christian Rosencreutz is the Western Branch of the Great White Lodge from which many occult groups in the Western Tradition depend, directly or indirectly.

The Tomb of Christian Rosencreutz
Central to the initial teaching which they released in the *Fama Fraternitatis* was a detailed description of the tomb of their founder Christian Rosencreutz. This tomb is described in terms that invest it with the properties of a great hidden mystery, both in the circumstances of its discovery and in the symbolic design of it. In this we have, in another form, the Mysteries of the centre of the magic circle or the Wheel of Death and Rebirth. These have remained the same since the Mysteries of antiquity. Indeed this is to be expected.

If the rose is at the centre of the cross, then the uncorrupted body of the Grand Master, Christian Rosencreutz, may also be found at the centre of this Mystery system. The tomb symbolism also contains the powerful dynamics of coming to terms with the principle of form. This we have already discussed in the mythology of the hero and of the old sea forces—Perseus and the Medusa; the Twelve Labours of Heracles and so forth. This element can be easily overlooked amid the quaint Baroque veil of the symbolism used in the Rosicrucian literature.

The discovery of the tomb appears to be by accident. In fact it has been pre-destined. This is revealed by certain singular events and apparent coincidences. This, as anyone with a modicum of first-hand esoteric experience will aver, is a hallmark of inner/outer plane mediation.

The circumstances of the discovery are that, after the death of Christian Rosencreutz, the succession of his office was handed on first to Fr. D. and then to Fr. A. who, on his death-bed, announced to his successor Fr. N. N. that a great discovery was shortly to be made. Fr. N. N. happened to be an architect (an interesting hint of the links with freemasonry) and decided to make some alterations to 'his building' before going on a journey. Accordingly he moved a memorial tablet of brass that recorded 'all the names of the brethren with some few other things'. This necessitated removing a great nail, which in turn revealed a hidden door, upon which was written the year, and the statement in great letters POST 120 ANNOS PATEBO— 'after 120 years I will be revealed'.

It is worth noting that this is an interior discovery. The reference to 'his building' on the part of Fr. N. N. is akin to the reference by Jesus to 'the temple' that would be raised within three days of its destruction. In other words in one sense it is the body of the adept—that is, the Temple of the Holy Spirit. In a corporate sense it is the very real corporate body of the group; and the secrecy surrounding it for at least a century is an example of the technique and necessity for secrecy at certain stages in occult operations. Just as a seed needs warmth and darkness and freedom from disturbance in order to germinate and grow, so do the creative seeds, sown upon another level in occult praxis.

Thus in a properly contacted group there is an outer expression of it in all the apparently separate physical bodies of its members, and on an inner level a common coming together of souls in mutual interest. In the Orient this is often referred to as the 'ashram'. Alternatively it may be described as being 'within the aura' of the group or of the Master.

Similarly the Masters, or any of the senior inner plane members of an extensive group, can experience expression by sympathetic connection with members of the group who are incarnate upon the physical plane.

This teaching is to be found also in orthodox Christian circles where, as Jesus taught, the members of the Church are all part of the one vine; and that where two or three are gathered together there is he in the midst of them. This is not an exclusive prerogative of Christianity or of any religious denomination, it is a simple fact of inner/outer plane dynamics.

So, removing a great nail which affixed a commemorative brass plate to an old wall, Fr. N. N. made a great discovery. There is an important lesson in this imagery for the esoteric student. It is not enough simply to learn the intellectual facts about esoteric philosophy, to have them affixed as if on a brass tablet in the mind. One must go beyond them, by practical experience, to what lies behind them. This entails a willingness for transformation, to be a rebuilder of one's own soul, eager to break down that which is no longer of use, and to reconstruct where called to do so. This removal of the nailed metallic plate to find the hidden door is likewise the finding of the centre of the magic circle of life experience.

After finding the hidden door, and undertaking the heavy work of removing obstructing old masonry, Fr. N. N. and his colleagues await for the dawn of a new day. They then pass within.

There they find an enclosed chamber which is, however, lit brightly as by an interior sun. This is a common statement of those who had penetrated the ancient Mysteries: that they had gone into the underworld and seen the sun shine at midnight; or had found the starry universe *within* rather than beyond the Earth.

The vault itself is a highly symbolic structure. It has seven sides and corners. Each side is 5 units broad and 8 units high. And in the centre stands a circular altar upon which is an engraved round brass plate.

The heptagonal ceiling is divided into triangles. At their common centre is an interior sun. The heptagonal floor is likewise divided but what is to be seen in each of the seven upper and seven lower triangles is not described. This is knowledge that individuals must discover for themselves. Each of the seven sides of the vault is divided into ten parts, each containing symbolic diagrams and descriptive sentences.

It may be assumed that the type of these wall diagrams is similar to the various Rosicrucian and alchemical diagrams of the Renaissance. The upper and lower triangles have particular correspondence to the seven modes of inner force in their upper and lower aspects. These are usually designated with traditional planetary names, and contain the sum total of spiritual love, strength and wisdom in the Universe, split into the seven rays of the spectrum of consciousness.

Each of the seven walls likewise has an enclosed chest containing appropriate magical books and instruments. The works of Paracelsus are particularly mentioned, and also magic mirrors ('looking glasses of diverse virtues') or crystal specula, bells, lamps and songs—seemingly disparate and pointless objects. However, a glass enables vision of other planes of being; a bell attracts the attention of beings on other levels; lamps act as a focus for spiritual work and the mediation of spiritual beings; and 'artificial songs' or songs of the magical art are the application of harmonic principles to group endeavour. Michael Maier, and other Rosicrucians of the period, spent much effort on creating symbolic canons and fugues.

The circular plate on the central altar bears a number of inscriptions in Latin: 'This compendium of the universe I made in my own lifetime to be my tomb' is prominently displayed, and then around the outermost rim: JESUS MIHI OMNIA—Jesus, my all, signifies the Christocentric intention of these Mysteries, as indeed the name of the Founder would imply.

Inside this are four circular figures each containing:

NEQUAQUAM VACUUM	A vacuum exists nowhere
LEGIS JUGUM	The Yoke of the Law
LIBERTAS EVANGELII	The Liberty of the Gospel
DEI GLORIA INTACTA	The Whole Glory of God

These together give the axiomatic principles of Rosicrucian philosophy. These are that the rule of God is everywhere in the Universe, and that the freedom of interpretation of holy writ and the book of nature is the only means to reveal the full majesty of God's universal laws.

The central mystery is, however, down in a further vault that is found only by penetrating beyond the central altar. Beneath this altar, which is removable, is to be found a brass trap-door set in the floor. Below this they find the body of Christian Rosencreutz, fair and uncorrupted, in full ceremonial regalia. In his hand is a parchment book that they consider to be the greatest literary treasure next to the Bible.

This book is one that each individual must seek to read by

personal endeavour. It concludes, however, with an elegaic paragraph describing Christian Rosencreutz as 'a grain buried in the breast of Jesus Christ'. In other words, his life and Mysteries are an esoteric development of Christianity, containing 'secrets of heaven and earth' obtained through 'divine revelations, subtle cogitations and unwearied toil'. Finding his treasure not suitable for the world of his own times he had constructed this 'compendium of things past, present and to come', it being 'a microcosm corresponding in all motions to the macrocosm'. Finally, although not afflicted by disease, he had been summoned to return his soul to God, and his incorruptible body was laid to rest to be discovered after 120 years.

According to further information given in the *Confessio* it can be computed that as he was born in 1378, and lived for 106 years, that is until 1484; his tomb was discovered in 1604, the year when two new stars appeared in the sky in the constellations of Cygnus—the Swan—and Serpentario—the Serpent.

In seventeenth-century esoteric symbolism there does tend to be a plethora of detail. Although none of it is without significance, it is necessary, at a distance of over three centuries, to realize that the greater detail (such as the initials and functions of the brethren) may prove more of a distraction than an enlightenment. It is necessary, therefore, to appreciate the general drift of the major symbolism and then to conduct one's own inner researches. Historians may quite validly debate the significance of, say, the year 1604, and whether this signified the date of formation of a particular esoteric organization such as the 'Militia Evangelica'. However, the deeper seeker will seek for the primary inner, rather than the secondary outer knowledge, and that has to be found within.

Thus, in the *Confessio* it is stated 'If there be some body now, which . . . will complain . . . that we offer our treasures so freely . . . those we do not contradict . . . but withall we signify . . . that our Arcana or secrets will no ways be common, and generally made known. Although the *Fama* be set forth in five languages . . . the unlearned and gross wits will not receive nor regard the same.'

Furthermore, 'the worthiness of those who shall be accepted into our Fraternity are not esteemed and known of as by Man's carefulness, but by the Rule of our Revelation and Manifestation . . . God hath so encompassed us about with his clouds, that unto us his servants no violence or force can be done or committed; wherefore we neither can be seen or known by anybody, except he had the eyes of an eagle.'

The 'eye of an eagle' is no mere figurative expression. It is a technical term for spiritual insight. The eagle traditionally is the only creature that can look directly at the Sun. In this instance the spiritual sun is signified, or the Sun at midnight of the ancient Mystery tradition.

In other words the Order is an inner plane one, and to be sought there. Although it will have certain delegates on the physical plane, functioning either as individuals or as small groups, they are but the external extension of the Brotherhood. They will not necessarily be in contact with one another, or even know of each other's existence.

Nor should all esoteric claimants to this tradition be taken at face value. The *Confessio* trenchantly states the position here: 'But to the false hypocrites, and to those that seek other things than wisdom, we say . . . we cannot be made known and be betrayed by them . . . but they shall certainly be partakers of all the punishment spoken of in our *Fama*; so their wicked counsels shall light upon themselves, and our treasures shall remain untouched and unstirred until the Lion doth come, who will ask them for his use, and employ them for the confirmation and establishment of his kingdom.'

The punishments referred to in the *Fama* are strictures against the attempted commercial exploitation of alchemical doctrine, described as 'the ungodly and accursed gold-making, which hath gotten so much the upper hand, whereby under colour of it, many renegates and roguish people do use great villanies and cozen and abuse the credit which is given them.'

This is not to say that the control of the Elementary world is a delusion, but rather that control for its own sake is a dangerous perversion of spiritual priorities. The true Rosicrucian 'doth not rejoice that he can make gold, and that, as Christ, the devils are obedient unto him; but is glad that he seeth the heavens open, and the angels of God ascending and descending, and his name written in the book of life.'

By getting the priorities right nothing but good can prevail, but to pervert the Mysteries of created existence brings great retribution. 'And this we say for a truth, that whosoever shall earnestly, and from his heart, bear affection unto us, it shall be beneficial to him in goods, body and soul; but he that is false-hearted, or only greedy of riches, the same first of all shall not be able in any manner or wise to hurt us, but bring himself to utter ruin and destruction.'

These are no light words but are an expression of the very real dangers that exist in tampering with the machinery of the universe without due dedication and guidance.

The inner plane nature of the Order is further made plain '. . . although at this time we make no mention either of names or meetings, yet nevertheless everyone's opinion shall assuredly come to our hands, in what language so ever it be.' In other words all desires of men are known to them. A sincere desire for enlightenment shines as a torch upon the inner planes. Following upon this, contact will assuredly be arranged, for, 'nor anybody shall fail, who so gives his name, but to speak with some of us either by word of mouth, or else, if there be some let, in writing.'

This may not be so very apparent as it sounds. The contact in the first instance may be simply in the form of apparently subjective mental impressions. Perhaps to read a particular book, to attend a particular meeting, to join a particular group, or undertake some particular venture—none of which may lead immediately to a specifically Rosicrucian contact. It may be, however, the first step of a number of steps towards such an overt contact. In the last analysis this leads to the ability to go within, for 'our building (although one hundred thousand people had very near seen and beheld the same) shall for ever remain untouched, undestroyed, and hidden to the wicked world.'

The treasures of the Rosicrucian Brotherhood are not for immediate material profit in this world but are for offering in the service of 'the Lion'. As we have already quoted, it is specifically stated in the *Confessio* that: 'our treasures shall remain untouched and unstirred until the Lion doth come, who will ask them for his use, and employ them for the confirmation and establishment of his kingdom.'

Who or what is this Lion?

According to one scholar it is mentioned in the 1617

Frankfurt edition of the *Confessio* where, three paragraphs previously, the pre-Reformation teachings of the Roman Church are likened to the braying of an ass, which will be replaced 'by a new voice', or alternatively 'by the new voice of a roaring lion'.

The general tenor of the *Confessio* is that of the wisdom and knowledge that will accrue on the correct interpretation of the Holy Bible. In this it is generally on the side of the Protestant movement, with an emphasis on the personal study of the Holy scriptures, rather than the hierarchical Roman Catholic position which puts greater emphasis on a priesthood mediating divine grace in the form of the sacraments, to the laity.

'. . . we do admonish everyone for to read diligently and continually the Holy Bible, for he that taketh all his pleasures therein, he shall know that prepared for himself an excellent way to come to our Fraternity.' The Holy Bible they regard indeed as 'a compendium and content of the whole world'.

At the same time the *Confessio* recognizes the danger, very prevalent in the early days of Protestantism, of many sectarians and fanatics reading into it their own prejudices. Thus: '. . . it is not our custom to prostitute and make so common the Holy Scriptures; for there are innumerable expounders of the same; some alleging and wresting it to serve for their opinion . . .' However, there is an inner meaning to the Holy Bible which is open to the wise. 'Blessed is he that hath the same; yet more blessed is he who reads it diligently, but most blessed of all is he that truly understandeth the same, for he is most like to God, and doth come most near to him.'

The true reading of Holy Writ is then closely associated with the coming of 'the Lion'.

Various interpretations have been put upon this, not least in popularity its identification with Frederick, the Elector Palatine and 'Winter King' of Bohemia in his struggle to form a Rosicrucian buffer state between Catholic and Protestant Europe. Whatever the validity of these historical theories, (and there no doubt were seventeenth-century enthusiasts of a political kind of Rosicrucianism, just as there were gold-seeking alchemically oriented Rosicrucian aspirants), there is an overriding esoteric validity to the symbolism which transcends political and proto-scientific interpretations.

In relation to the Lion this is to be found particularly in the work of Christopher Kotter, a Protestant clergyman of Bohemia, and his account of a series of visions he had between 1616 and 1624. These visions were highly thought of in influential esoteric circles of the time. The Bohemian reformer and educationalist Comenius quoted them at length in his book *Lux in Tenebris* (published in 1657), and personally brought them to the attention of King Frederick, when in exile at the Hague, in 1626.

Of particular interest are the engravings, two of which are reproduced in Frances Yates' *The Rosicrucian Enlightenment.* This book is a valuable and interesting account of the possible political interpretation. However the esoteric indications are, in our view, of far greater significance.

This is particularly so in the image of the lion. This is first seen standing before an orb on the ground and preparing, sword in hand, to fight a snake, whilst above them, high in the sky, is a star. Then the lion is shown triumphant, holding the orb, and with radiant head, whilst the star is to be seen, flaming, on the ground, whilst the snake is raised up into the sky, cut in four pieces. This process is being witnessed by three men sitting under a tree at the edge of a wood.

Another plate shows presumably the same three men sitting at a table with their hands clasped in a circle. Before each one of them a rose appears, and in the centre a rampant lion. Under the table top on one of its supports is an equal armed cross.

Other visions of Kotter included a lion with four heads, and a lion standing on a moon embraced by six other lions.

An esoteric interpretation of this is that the lion is the serpent power raised to a higher level—by a process of balancing the four elemental powers, and by development from the moon powers in conjunction with the other six 'planetary' forces. This raising of the planetary Kundalini, so to speak, reverses the usual conception of the universal order. That which seemed heavenly and remote (the star), is brought as a source of light and power to earth. That which seemed evil (the serpent), is overcome; and its essential force, freed from crawling on its belly on the earth, is raised up.

There is obviously a connection between this lion and serpent symbolism and that of the lionskin-clad Heracles and the serpentine monsters that he was called upon to overcome. It is also relevant to the coming to terms with the feminine. This fact is not overtly stated, but it becomes the more obvious the closer one works with the symbolism of the third Rosicrucian tract *The Chymical Marriage of Christian Rosencreutz.*

The Chymical Marriage of Christian Rosencreutz

This symbolic story commences on Easter Eve, with all its connotations of transformation and resurrection. The protagonist, who is called Christian Rosencreutz, is approached by a fair glorious lady. She wears sky coloured garments spangled with stars, and has beautiful wings full of eyes, like a peacock's tail. She is obviously a form of the Heavenly Isis—Isis Urania—the heavenly or cosmic aspect of the feminine principle. She carries a bundle of letters in all languages and a golden trumpet. She leaves Christian Rosencreutz a letter, which is an invitation to a wedding, and departs with a resounding blast of her trumpet.

Christian Rosencreutz, or C.R., dreams that night that he is confined in a dark underground dungeon. It is packed with other prisoners who swarm all over each other, regardless of inflicting injury. Their overriding desire is to heave themselves over others. In short it is an image of the outer world.

Trumpets and drums sound and the cover of the dungeon is lifted. The prisoners scramble toward the light and an old man speaks to them from above. He tells them that if they would be less selfish and self-centred *his mother* could help them the more.

As it is, a cord can be let down seven times, and whoever can cling to it will be released. There is a mad scramble to seize the descending rope but C.R. is successful without joining in this mêlée, for he earnestly prays to God for help. At this the rope swings toward him. He happens to be standing at the side on a great stone and so can clasp the rope. The stone is significant of his standpoint on the rock of faith and, more esoterically, it is the outermost form of the stone of the philosophers.

As he is drawn up however, his head strikes on another sharp stone and is wounded. The significance of this wound is recounted later. It is concerned with the force of love—and even at the shallowest level of interpretation the treasures of the heart are shown to be paramount over the analysis of the head.

The names of all those who are saved are written on a golden tablet and they are freed from their chains and given a piece of gold. Upon this is inscribed a sun at dawn, and the inscription D.L.S. This is variously interpreted as Deus Lux Solis (God is the Light of the Sun), and/or as Deo Laus Semper (God be praised for ever). There is always a tone of reverence in genuine Rosicrucian documents. Knowledge is not elevated into a self-sufficient false god. Hence these teachings conform to the old principle of the Mysteries that the candidate for initiation must genuinely be able to say: 'I desire to know in order to serve'.

The old man can be equated with Saturn—the outermost of the traditional planets and so guardian of the bounds of the Solar System. That is, Lord of its space and time. His mother is older even than he. She is in fact, by definition, the most ancient feminine principle, who *was* before all worlds. Yet she is not a remote abstraction or unapproachable deity. She laments for all the poor souls left in the dungeon and enters into a personal relationship with all who are saved, each of whom is presented to her.

She consoles C.R. for the wounds he has received from his earthly chains, yet at the same time laughing at him. This is not a callous laughter but that of a loving mother, for from the heavenly viewpoint these wounds are but the scrapes and scratches of cosmic childhood. The lesson is not to dwell in self-pity upon them but to be thankful for blessings and to regard these wounds as badges of experience. 'My son,' she says, 'let not this defect afflict thee,' as he stands fancying himself unable to proceed, 'but call to mind thy infirmities, and therewith thank God who hath permitted thee even in this world, and in the state of thy imperfection to come into so high a light, and keep these wounds for my sake.'

The trumpets then sound, and they have the usual effect of esoteric trumpets in that they call those who hear them from one plane to another. Accordingly C.R. awakes.

He determines to attend the wedding and dresses ritually for it. That is, with the emblems of a Rosicrucian—a crossed red ribbon over a white linen coat and with four red roses in his hat. In other words, the centre of the cross is over his heart, and the equilibration of the elements blossoms over his head.

He takes bread, salt and water—all emblems of life—and

typically, and essentially, for the aspirant to the higher mysteries, gives thanks to God. The principle of thanksgiving is of incredible power at any level of expression. He also vows that whatever is revealed to him he will use in the service of God and his fellow man. He then goes into the forest, with birds singing all around him, as in a dawn chorus.

All initiation systems have an especial commencement point. This is often associated with a tree or a grove of trees. In this case it is a green plain beyond the forest from which four ways diverge. It is marked by three tall cedar trees which offer 'an excellent and desired shade'. One is indeed reminded of the Rosicrucian motto which appears at the end of the *Confessio* SUB UMBRA ALARUM TUUM JEHOVA—Under the shadow of thy wings Jehovah. Under the trees is a tablet describing the nature of the four ways. In fact only three are practicable, for the fourth is passable only by the pure—that is, by those with incorruptible bodies.

The right choice is beyond the powers of intellect, and C.R. elects upon the right way by apparent accident. This is significantly by the actions of a black raven—an emblem found in alchemy as a symbol for dissolution. It is a bird ever associated both with wisdom and with death. It is found in ancient Irish myth as the Morrigu, the great terrible goddess of the battlefield, who collects the souls of the slain. C.R. sees a white dove and begins to feed it with his bread, whereupon the black raven appears and chases the dove, which flies off towards the south. C.R. runs after them, to find himself automatically upon one of the ways and unable to return for his bread and belongings, by dint of a strong wind that blows from behind him. This is the breath of the Holy Spirit, whose other aspect is the guiding dove.

C.R. keeps to the path with the aid of a compass. This is an important symbolic direction-finding instrument. The lodestone (which is often meteoric in origin, and therefore literally from the heavens) is a natural object that automatically seeks the direction of the polar axis about which all the universe spins.

At sunset he comes to a stately portal. It is the first of three gates, and at each of these he receives a token. First in exchange for his water and his salt, and at the last gate he loses a part of his coat.

The first gate is surmounted by the traditional warning cry of the guardian of ancient mystery rites 'Begone, profane ones'. It is also surrounded by an orchard. Thus within this very baroque symbol structure we find mystery symbolism of great antiquity, for the orchard is to be found also in the Garden of Eden and in the Garden of the Hesperides, to say nothing of the Celtic Avalon or Isle of Apples.

Added to this, a virgin robed in celestial blue lights lanterns on every third tree. In a sense she can be looked upon as a celestial angel lighting the stars that appear in the heavens. This is an image of very considerable significance for it is the all comprehending feminine power.

At the second gate C.R. is confronted by the familiar figure of a roaring lion. At first it is grim and frightening but when confronted with pure dedication, it no longer threatens.

C.R. has to hasten to the last gate, in increasing darkness, but is aided by a feminine figure, the celestial Virgin of Lights. She runs with him and behind him, affording light for him to run by, until he reaches sanctuary between the two pillars of the final portal.

Here his name is recorded and is sent to the Bridegroom of the mysterious marriage. He is also given a new pair of shoes with which to walk the marble floor of the castle. This signifies activity upon a higher plane and is the reason why special shoes are ritually worn by those who tread in holy temples. In Qabalistic terms the magical weapons of Yesod, the etheric/astral sphere of the Tree of Life are sandals. They signify the means to walk the inner ways.

The hair of C.R.'s head is then cut into a tonsure. This is an indication of the opening of the crown chakra, the spiritual centre of the aura, called in the East the 1,000 petalled lotus. He is then left to meditate between two flaming torches struck into holes in the floor, like flaming pillars of an inner gateway.

Then he is taken to a banquet in a great hall where many others are present. A number of them consider they are there by right of their own merit rather than through the grace of God. They laugh at what they consider the over-pious humility of C.R. and see no need of God in their endeavours. They even wink and make fun during the saying of grace, and continue through the feast to boast of their esoteric accomplishments.

However this is curbed when a beautiful music commences. These are evidently heavenly harmonies for they impel silence even upon the most ignorant and garrulous, who are physically struck into silence.

This is the prelude to trumpets and drums outside and the amazing spectacle of a procession of thousands of little lighted tapers, like stars. They accompany two pages clad in sparkling white and gold robes who hold pillar-like flaming torches before the Virgin of Lights. She is similarly robed and seated in glory upon a moving golden throne. This is another aspect of the great cosmic figure represented by the Virgin of Lights in the orchard and is worthy of much meditation and reverent contemplation.

She announces that all who seek to attend the wedding must be weighed in the balance to see if they be found worthy. Those who feel that they are unworthy, however, will be allowed to sleep on the floor of the hall and will be given release on the morrow to return to their homes. Most of those present assume that they are self-evidently worthy and are conducted to their chambers.

C.R., however, feels that he is unworthy of such great and holy mysteries and, with eight others, elects to remain, bound and in darkness, in the discomfort of the hall, where they are enjoined to silence.

The next day the guests return to the hall, some of them deriding C.R. and the others for lacking the will and courage to submit to the forthcoming test. There follows a further tattoo of trumpets and drums, and the Virgin re-enters. She now wears scarlet velvet, relieved by a white scarf, and has a laurel wreath on her head. She is an image of power and justice and her throne is hauled by two hundred men, who are also clad in red and white and bear swords and ropes. On descending from her throne, she congratulates those who have remained in the hall all night as being 'sensible to your wretched condition'. She shows however amused surprise at finding C.R. among them, for, as it turns out, he is far more worthy than the whole concourse of seekers; a fact which is apparently quite obvious to her.

Great gold scales are erected and each one of the company is weighed in turn, to see if their spiritual weight is sufficient. This is a test very similar to that found in the Egyptian Book of the Dead, where the soul is weighed in the Judgment Hall of Osiris to determine its inner world fate. To their dismay, the majority of those present fail—even those who try to make themselves weighty by heavy books. Nor does wealth or rank serve to help any of them.

The few who pass the test are clad in scarlet, and given a laurel wreath, like the Virgin, and permitted to sit on the steps of her throne.

Even those who elected to stay in the hall are in fact weighed, though without risk of retribution should they fail the test. C.R., indeed, to his great surprise, proves to be of greatest spiritual weight, and accordingly is allowed to release one of the captives. He chooses to assist one who had shown great humility despite having high earthly rank, and who had only just failed the test.

The Virgin then presides over the judgment of those who failed and punishments are meted out accordingly to the gap between their pretensions and their actual performance. Those who had remained in humility in the hall risk no retribution. The swindling esoteric charlatans are most savagely punished. For most of those present the worse punishment is the realization of their lack of real worth in the scale of spiritual values, and their consequent banishment from the higher degrees of the mysteries of attendance at the wedding.

In all these events it is the Virgin who is mistress of the ceremonies and she is, in this role, an aspect of divine justice, and pictorially she resembles the Tarot Trump Justice. She presides over the ceremony at noon when those not worthy to take further part are dismissed from the company. They return to the outer world, after having drunk a draft of forgetfulness. This is similar to Lethe, the river of forgetfulness, found in the classical conception of the divide between the inner and outer worlds. This means that there is normally no memory of past lives before the present birth or of the inner life in the hours of sleep.

Of considerable importance in this sequence, although easily overlooked in the welter of symbolism, is the fact that this process of dividing the worthy from the unworthy, at the border between inner and outer levels, takes place in a garden around a fountain. The fountain, together with a garden, orchard, or grove of trees, is an almost invariable feature of entrances to the inner planes in esoteric mythology.

The fountain has upon it as its guardian a lion holding a sword, a symbolic creature with which we have already become familiar. After the unworthy have been dismissed there is a pregnant silence within the garden. This silence in itself is a mighty symbol. It is the stillness of the great feminine archetype, whether in the silence of the Sephirah Binah on the Tree of Life, the great temple of form of all the spheres; or in the great silent Unmanifest Sea of the Ain Soph beyond Kether, the ultimate feminine principle.

In the silence a unicorn approaches wearing a golden collar. It bows to the lion. The lion thereupon breaks the sword in two, and casts the pieces into the waters of the fountain. The testing having been done, the way to the higher worlds is clear, and the lion no longer bars the way. The roaring lion in the path, the Dweller on the Threshold or Shadow Self, is no longer a barrier to progress. A white dove now appears with an olive branch of peace and wisdom. The lion devours it and is quieted, and the unicorn joyfully departs.

All present then descend by a winding stair, and wash their hands and heads in the waters of eternal life of the fountain. The departing Virgin announces that they will meet the King on the morrow.

For the rest of the day the wedding guests are free to explore the castle, each guided by their individual page. One of the principle things to be seen is a library containing a great catalogue of all the contents of the castle, but more important than this, it is said, is a royal sepulchre from which may be learned *more than is extant in all books.* It is covered with many symbolic sculptures including that of a lion, an eagle, a griffon and a falcon, but above all by a glorious phoenix.

This is an important passage. The page allocated to each guest is in one sense an inner guide, in another a form of the holy guardian angel of each one, or an aspect of the Higher Self. In practical terms it is often difficult to differentiate between these categories of contact with the outer world personality; they function similarly, and with the same intent. Certainly, however, for the personality to tread the inner pathways, some form of guidance is needed.

There is on the outer levels of the inner Mysteries a great source of knowledge that is sometimes referred to as a great library. It is, in another sense and form, the akashic record, that is impressed with all occurrences in the world as a kind of reflecting ether with a permanent after-image. This knowledge of all conditions and events is there for those enabled to read it. However, of greater importance is not the record of the past but the secrets of the present and future state of the soul. The knowledge and wisdom of this is to be found in a tomb, moreover a tomb upon which is prominently displayed the image of the phoenix—the bird of resurrection and transformation.

It should be said that totem animals formed an extremely important part in the mystery beliefs of our remote ancestors. They remain important in folk lore and mythology, whether in the animal-headed gods of the Egyptians or in the creatures of fairy-tales that often give guidance into hidden realms or bring aid or information. Thus more attention might well be paid to the mythical creatures that appear in Rosicrucian and alchemical symbolism. They are guides and bearers of forces and influences beyond the normal frontiers of human cognition.

Another symbol of considerable importance that is here mentioned is a terrestrial globe, thirty feet in diameter, which serves a dual function. One is of indicating the position in the world of all initiates by the presence of gold rings set thereon. More importantly, the globe also opens up so that one can enter inside the Earth. There, on the inside, is a planetarium, with all the stars of the universe *inside* the earth.

This is a very ancient world view, that may seem ludicrous to modern habits of thought, yet which has a profound validity of its own. It is interesting to see this represented, almost in passing, in a seventeenth-century document that ostensibly seems to be merely revelling in mechanical contrivances. In fact the whole Rosicrucian castle is represented as a model driven by clockwork. It is indeed a moveable representation of the 'machinery of the universe', the inner world of the astro-etheric that keeps the outer world in order and motion.

The real force that drives the 'machinery of the universe' is however the topic of much riddling conversation at supper that evening, which is how to measure love. That night C.R. dreams of a locked door finally opening. We are indeed at the threshold of the Mysteries of the feminine principle at the centre of the magic circle.

The following day all those accepted to the Mysteries return to the golden fountain. The lion now bears a tablet of instruction in place of the sword. 'Drink of me who can: wash in me whoever so wishes: stir me whoever dares.' The waters are revealed to be those of Hermes—that is, higher wisdom, an analogue of the powers of Pallas Athene who helped the ancient heroes. The final injunction is 'Drink brethren, and live'. In other words, all who have achieved to this point *are* able to drink of these waters of higher wisdom; to take them within themselves. And the ability so to do makes them part of a great brotherhood, as well as bestowing conscious participation in a higher or eternal life.

This is ratified, after they have drunk from the golden cup of the fountain and washed therein, by their being conducted by the Virgin of Lights into a hall. Here they are decked in gold robes decorated with flowers, given a golden fleece set with jewels, and also a gold medal depicting the sun and moon conjoined. This indicates the union of higher and lower self, and the glory of the unmanifest spirit flowing through the conjunction. A more common depiction of this is by two equilateral triangles conjoined to form a radiant six-rayed star. The motto on the reverse of the medal confirms this:

The light of the Moon shall be as the light of the Sun,
and the light of the Sun shall be 7 times lighter.

They then process, with stately harmonies, up a winding staircase of 365 steps (the number of revolutions of the Earth in circumambulating the Sun), go through a painted arch at the top (the arch of heaven familiar to certain freemasons), to find themselves in an upper hall decked like paradise. Here they are greeted by sixty virgins bearing laurel wreaths. Each of the initiates is also given a laurel wreath by the Virgin of Lights. She then presents each one of them to the King of the castle who, with the Queen, is revealed behind a curtain. The Queen, it should be said, is clad in garments so brilliant that the eye cannot look upon them.

The Virgin of Lights lays down her branch upon the ground and silence falls upon the assembled company. In this holy quietness the figure of Atlas steps forth and welcomes them on the king's behalf. Again we find ourselves in the presence of most ancient symbolism. Atlas is one of the Titans, and particularly associated with the Hesperides, from whom Heracles sought aid in obtaining the golden apples. One of his functions is also to uphold the sphere of the heavens.

Atlas then bids the Virgin to continue the ceremonies, and we note that these mysteries are run by feminine forces. She leads the company to another room where, under a great arch in the West, are three royal thrones. Each throne has a couple seated upon it, with a semi-circle of elders behind them, and a great golden crown over all. The central throne bears a young couple, the bride and bridegroom of the Mystery wedding, and a figure of Cupid plays about them and round the golden crown. We should by now be aware that the figure of Cupid is no sentimental convention, but represents an almighty force that drives the worlds in their motions and fires the vital forces of all living creatures upon them.

Before the Queen is an altar, dressed with symbols relating to the Mysteries about to be encountered. These are a black velvet book inlaid with gold; a taper in an ivory candlestick; a celestial globe; a striking watch; a fountain of blood; and a skull wherein dwells a white serpent.

Each of these symbols will repay long and deep meditation. They are each in their way aspects of the Mystery dynamics of life and death, of transformation and regeneration. The intention of such symbolism is to reveal not to explain, and although it may seem obscure it is in fact not so. It is the plainest possible representation of a truth that is beyond the grasp of the intellect. A symbol is a door or gateway. It is to be gone through. By meditating upon, visualizing, taking the symbol to heart, with aspiration and spiritual intention, one is enabled to pass through it.

Returning in procession to the lower hall the virgins play a game with the candidates which is based on the number 7. They all stand in a circle and count round in sevens, to choose bedfellows for the night. In doing so, however, they find they are so disposed by sexes round the circle that all the virgins are counted out first, leaving the men standing alone. This is an indication that these mysteries are connected with the sexual forces but not in the usual physical expression of them.

Cupid then reappears with a golden cup. They all drink from it and dance before forming up in procession again, led by the Queen. She carries a small crucifix of pearl, which is imbued with great significance, for it is said that it was 'this very day wrought between the young King and his Bride'. We say no more than to provide the hint that the crucifix is the paramount symbol of vicarious sacrifice and that pearl represents by its appearance a solidification of the life forces. This is sometimes referred to as the 'gluten of the white eagle', more familiar to nineteenth-century psychical research in the form of 'ecto-plasm', or more subtle etheric forms of it.

The Queen is attended by six virgins who bear the symbols from the little altar, referred to now as the 'King's jewels'. The three kings and three queens follow, with the bride and bridegroom in black, and Cupid bearing the bride's train. They are followed by the rest of the company with Atlas bringing up the rear.

They go to a theatre called the House of the Sun and there witness a play in seven acts. This enacts the story of a maiden disinherited and then seduced by a wicked Moorish king. She is rescued by a king's son to be his bride, but falls again perversely and willingly into the evil king's clutches. She is then sadly degraded by him. The young king battles for her again in spite of her defection. Although it appears at first that he is killed, he in fact has the victory and commits his intended bride to the safe keeping of a steward and a chaplain. These two subsequently become insolently wicked in the exercise of their appointed power. They are overthrown by the young king in the last act, who then marries his bride.

All of this is an allegory of Christ and the human soul. Saved once more by the Incarnation of the Christ the soul of humanity is put under the stewardship of the Church, which however betrays its trust in hubris and ambition. It is prophesied that this will be overturned at the final coming of the Christ.

As Dante three hundred years before, in the pageant in the *Earthly Paradise*, allegorized the institutional Church as betraying its spiritual trust in search of political power, so do the Rosicrucian documents, and plainly demonstrate themselves to be on the side of the Reformation.

After the play a banquet is held, for the most part in an

awesome silence as if portending some great event. At its end all sign a book, dedicating themselves to the King's service. They then drink a 'draught of silence'.

A bell tolls. The rest of the royal party put off their festive white garments and are clad in black. The Queen blindfolds them and six coffins are brought in. A tall black man enters with an axe and beheads each one of them. The blood is caught in a gold cup and the heads wrapped in black cloths. Finally the executioner is himself beheaded, by an unknown hand at the door.

The Virgin of Lights bids the company not to lament. She enigmatically states that the lives of those beheaded even yet rest in the hands of the assembled company.

All retire for the night, but at midnight C.R. looks out of his window. He sees over the lake seven ships proceeding with the coffins, each one with a flame over its mast-head.

At dawn the next day, which is the wished for day of the intended wedding, C.R., is secretly shown some very significant hidden mysteries of the castle by his guiding Page.

First they go down an underground stairway where they find a great iron door. Upon it is inscribed in letters of copper, 'Here lies buried Venus, that beauty which hath undone many a great man both in fortune, honour, blessing and prosperity'.

Beyond the door is a dark passage which leads to a small door. This, the Page reveals, was first opened only the day before, to bring out the coffins. It has since remained open. We are on the threshold of deep Mysteries of love and the creative principle revealed only by sacrifice.

Within the little door is a marvellous vault, lit by the glow of precious jewels. This, C.R. is told, is the King's Treasure. We may recall that to reach this place we have come an underground way, and that in Greek mythology the King of the Underworld is associated with great riches.

The main wonder of the place is a central sepulchre, fantastically adorned with precious jewels and of a peculiar and significant shape.

It is triangular, which Qabalists will recognize as the principle of form, and has a great polished copper bowl at its centre. Within the burnished copper bowl stands an angel, holding in his arms a strange and mysterious tree, from which the fruit fall into the bowl. As they do so they liquefy and run into three small golden bowls standing by. These form a little altar, supported by an eagle, an ox and a lion. These are three of the Holy Living Creatures of the Vision of Ezekiel. They are normally four in number, the fourth being represented by a man or an angel—who in this instance may be identified with the angelic figure in the central copper bowl.

The Page then repeats the message that was found in mysterious copper script on the outer iron door, and shows C.R. a copper trap-door set into the floor of the vault. They go through it and descend into pitch darkness. The Page opens a little chest to reveal a perpetual light (ever a symbol of the inmost spirit and source of our being) with which he lights a torch by which they can see.

C.R. is overtaken by great fear at their temerity in advancing so far into these hidden Mysteries, but the Page assures him that all is safe as long as the sacrificed royal persons are still at rest.

He then shows C.R. a great bed hung about with rich curtains. Drawing one of these aside, and heaving up the coverlets, he suddenly reveals that which in the ancient Mysteries was held to be unknowable and unseeable by mortal man. That is, the naked form of Lady Venus—or Isis Unveiled.

She is in fact sleeping, which may explain the Page's remark that this is a unique occasion and opportunity. It is a time in the process of sacrifice and regeneration when all is quiescent; and the dynamics involved may be revealed to the rare soul who is worthy to see them.

Over the bed of the sleeping Venus is a tablet inscribed with an esoteric script. The Page declines to translate it, saying that C.R. will learn its import through his own experience. In fact it says, 'When the fruit shall be quite melted down then I shall awake and be the mother of a King'.

The Page extinguishes the torch after drawing the covers again, and they climb back to the vault of the triangular sepulchre. C.R. is now the better able to examine the place and sees that the tree is melted by heat radiated from the shining precious stones in the walls. These to clearer sight seem to be not only precious stones but mineral tapers burning with a uniquely clear fire. The tree, as it melts in their heat, continually produces new fruit.

The Page then tells C.R. what was written above the bed of the Lady Venus, and that this information emanates from Atlas. At this precise moment the little Cupid flies in and discovers them. It is plainly a matter of great enormity that someone has penetrated to these depths, and come so close to discovering the sleeping Venus. Cupid hastily seals the copper trap-door. C.R. and his Page do not dare admit that they have in fact penetrated into the *sanctum sanctorum.* Even so the Cupid says that he must punish C.R., at least in token, for coming so close to his mother's couch. Accordingly he pricks C.R. on the hand with one of his darts, which he has heated in one of the glowing stones that provide the heat for the transformation of the magical tree. This draws a drop of blood from C.R.'s hand.

There is more to come as a result of this incident, for it is pregnant with hidden meaning. Cupid, jesting, bids the others take good care of C.R. as his wound will soon bring him to the end of his days. By this he means not physical death but the death of initiation.

Serious mysteries may be describable only in terms of paradox, or in what passes for jest. Cupid continues to jest and make merry during the following funeral arrangements. Indeed jesting deception is the rule in the ceremonies that follow. The six coffins are solemnly laid in a sepulchre, even though from his observations of the night before C.R. knows them to be empty. Thus all the funeral pomp is a charade.

The coffins are laid in a wooden edifice of seven columns surmounted with a crown and a flag depicting a phoenix. The fact that the building is of wood, rather than the gold and jewels we have come to expect, suggests that it is a mere emblematic show. As the phoenix flag is raised, the Virgin of Lights tells them that if they are constant in their endeavours the dead will rise. To this end she bids them go with her to the Tower of Olympus.

She leads them through a little door to the shore, where seven little ships await them. They sail off in one of them surrounded by the other six, displaying planetary symbols. Saturn leads and Venus brings up the rear. To either side of them are Mercury and Mars, and immediately behind them the ships representing Sun and Moon.

They pass over the inland lake, and then into a narrow

channel which leads to the open sea. These decriptions have their analogues in the structure of human consciousness. As they strike the open sea they find themselves surrounded by creatures of the deep—sea nymphs, sirens, sea goddesses.

The seven ships are drawn up in formation. The two representing Sun and Moon remain in the centre whilst the other five stand about them. Saturn opposite Venus, Mars opposite Mercury, and that representing Earth, upon which the candidates ride, at the head of this five-sided figure. Apart from the significance of the Pentagram as a sigil of the power of the spirit over the Elements there is also in the disposition of the ships a correspondence with the slain couples. The Sun and Moon represent bridegroom and bride; Saturn and Venus represent the old king with the fair young queen; and Mars and Mercury the dark middle-aged king with the veiled uncrowned beautiful matron as his consort, representing the *materia* of transformation that is to be paired with the fiery, transformatory alchemical process.

The sea creatures present to the company, in honour of the wedding, a 'costly great, set, round and orient pearl, the like to which hath not at any time been seen, either in ours, or yet in the new world'. Plainly this is a very special mystery from the depths. It is a recognition of the transformation process and marriage about to be performed, and not unconnected with the pearl crucifix in the possession of the Queen, that had been wrought between the royal bride and groom. The assembled sea nymphs and goddesses then sing in delicate sweet voices a hymn to love.

Despite the allurements to stay, the presiding Virgin of Lights gives to the sea creatures, by way of return, a red scarf—an emblem of corporeal life—and the little fleet passes on. C.R. realizes that the wound on his hand he received from Cupid is the same as the blow to the head he received from a sharp stone in his initial dream.

They approach a square island surrounded by a thick wall. Within it is a fine meadow with little gardens containing strange fruits. In the centre a great round tower of seven stories. An ancient warden of the Tower comes to greet them in a golden pinnace, attended by guards in white.

They are taken to the base of the Tower of Olympus in which

they find a laboratory, and they are set to labour preparing juices and essences. Rude mattresses are slung on the floor for them to sleep on at night.

Before retiring however, C.R. wanders outside and stands on the top of the wall surrounding the island. He sees in the bright moonlight that the planets in the night sky are about to form a most rare conjunction. Then, as the clock strikes midnight, seven flames pass over the sea to the top of the tower. The winds rise suddenly, the sea becomes rough and threatening, and the moon disappears behind clouds. C.R. hurries back in from the tempestuous dark and lies down on his mattress. He is lulled to sleep by the gentle purling of a fountain that is in the laboratory.

The following day is taken up with a detailed alchemical process on successive levels of the Tower of Olympus. This is entirely under the direction of the Virgin of Lights, assisted by maidens and musicians. At the commencement of each stage she opens a trap-door in the ceiling and bids them ascend to her level. They do this according to their ability and temperament, figuratively described as some climbing ladders, others ropes, while a few have wings.

On the floor they tend a fountain-like apparatus in which are distilled the bodies of the sacrificed ones. The heat for this operation is generated from the executioner's head. A deep yellow essence distilled from this process is collected in a golden globe.

On the second floor the globe is heated in a room of mirrors. They concentrate the rays of the sun upon it from all angles. Eventually it shines as brightly as the sun itself and when it cools they open it with a sharp pointed diamond. This reveals a snow white egg.

On the third floor the egg is warmed in a square copper sand bath. A chick hatches from it which they feed with the blood of the beheaded ones, collected on the day of execution, diluted with liquid that they have prepared. The bird grows very quickly. At first it is black and fierce but then moults and becomes tamer, growing snow white feathers. Finally its feathers become multi-coloured and beautiful, though the head remains white. It is now very tame and they release it.

On the fourth floor they prepare a bath for the bird in a liquid coloured with white powder to resemble milk. The bird drinks some of the milky liquid and appears pleased with it. Lamps are placed under the bath and a lid placed over the top with a space for the bird's head to emerge. The bird's feathers boil off until it is as smooth as a baby, the dissolving feathers turning the liquid blue. The bird is led up and down, smooth and glittering, wearing a gold collar and chain. The blue liquid is meanwhile boiled away to precipitate a blue stone. This is ground down on a stone and used as a tincture to paint the bird's body blue—though still leaving the head white.

On the fifth floor they find an altar identical to the one before the Queen in the hall with its six symbolic objects—the book, the taper, the globe, the striking watch, the red fountain, and the skull with a white serpent.

The bird is added as a seventh object. It drinks from the blood red fountain and pecks the white serpent, which bleeds copiously. The blood is caught in a cup and then poured down the bird's reluctant throat. The serpent is revived by dipping its head in the fountain, and disappears into the skull. The celestial globe on the altar turns successively to those particular stellar configurations or conjunctions and the watch strikes one, then two, then three. The bird lays its head on the gold-tooled black velvet book, willingly allowing its head to be struck off by one of the assembled company who is chosen by lot. No blood flows until the bird's breast is opened. Then it spurts forth like a fountain of rubies. A fire is kindled and the bird's body is burnt to ashes. These are cleansed and laid in a box of cypress wood. C.R. and three other selected ones are taken up secretly to a further stage from which the others are now debarred. These others tend an alchemical furnace and assume that the transmutation of elements on the seventh floor is the highest mystery.

However C.R. and his three companions are instructed in a higher mystery by an old man who tends a small round furnace. He instructs them to moisten the bird's ashes with the prepared water until it is like thin dough; to heat this over the fire and then cast it into two moulds. They thus produce two little transparent images as fair as the body of the sleeping Venus. These are placed on satin cushions and fed from a gold cup with drops of blood of the bird.

The two figures grow and are placed on a long table of white velvet covered to the breast with a white cloth. Eventually they become of full human size. The old man covers their faces with a white silk cloth, torches are placed about the table, and the Virgin of Lights brings in crystalline garments which are laid by them.

Above the figures are seven concentric hemispheres. The topmost one has an opening in it but this is, however, closed.

Six virgins appear with large trumpets wreathed about with green glittering flaming material. The old man removes the face cloths and three times places a trumpet to the mouth of each figure. The wreath bursts into flames, the source of fire coming, as lightning, through the opening in the roof of the tower, and bringing life to the figures. Though only C.R. sees the true source of the flame.

All lights are extinguished. The figures are enwrapped in the velvet cloths and left to sleep. Meanwhile the brethren on the seventh floor have succeeded in preparing transmuted gold.

Finally Cupid comes to awaken the couple. They think they have slept since the beheading. They are dressed in the crystalline garments and adorned with gold chains. All then descend by a winding stair to a waiting ship upon which the Royal couple embark, attended by Cupid and some of the virgins.

The company is then entertained by the old warden of the Tower of Olympus. He conducts them through many secret chambers in the walls surrounding the island. Within them are many wondrous devices 'which man's wit in imitation of nature had invented'.

The Lord himself is also a master of wisdom and instructs them all profoundly on diverse matters. Finally, wearied of learning, they sleep in stately rooms within the walls, lulled to sleep by the gentle sound of the surrounding sea.

On the seventh and final day they have some difficulty in finding their way out through the labyrinthine corridors within the walls. Finally however they do so and are invested with yellow robes and their golden fleeces. The Virgin of Lights tells them that they are now Knights of the Golden Stone.

Each one receives a gold medal upon which are inscribed abbreviations of Latin mottos. 'Ars Naturae Ministra' and 'Temporis Natura Filia', which mean 'Art is the Priestess of

Nature' and 'Nature is the Daughter of Time'. The Warden of the Tower exhorts them ever to bear these principles in mind in all their works. The need for man's ingenuity to follow in the footsteps of nature is a precept that is a feature of Rosicrucian and alchemical literature, and a hallmark of the new learning advocated by Francis Bacon. Much can also be read into the second phrase. It has regard to the great phases of terrestrial revolution in which the movements of the earth itself are akin to a simple cog in a great universal clock.

The company embark upon twelve ships for their return journey. Each ship sails under the banner of one of the signs of the Zodiac. The one upon which C.R. and his fellow initiates sail is dedicated to Libra, whose ruling planet is Venus, and which signifies Balance, between Scorpio and the Virgin.

Upon their ship is to be found, prominently placed, a wondrous clock. The sea upon which they sail is now perfectly calm, and they are enthralled by the discourses of the Warden of the Tower.

The twelve ships are met by a great welcoming fleet awaiting them in the lake. Atlas makes an oration which is answered by the Warden of the Tower, who hands over a mysterious casket containing wedding gifts for the royal couple. This is placed in the keeping of Cupid.

As they disembark each is personally greeted by the young king and queen. They form a horseback procession and C.R. finds himself accompanied by no less than the Warden of the Tower and the young king.

Each one bears a snow white ensign upon which is a red cross. C.R. also wears upon his hat the gold tokens that he originally received at the threefold gates of the castle.

Attention is drawn to the similarity between C.R. and the Warden of the Tower. Both have long grey beards and hair. This is commonly a symbolic indication of great wisdom. The King also makes the cryptic remark, disguised as a jest, that C.R. is his father. He also remarks, on hearing about the episode of the dove, the raven and the bread, that C.R. is obviously not only very wise but under the blessing of God.

At this point they approach the gates of the castle where the Porter, clothed in blue, awaits them. He bears a supplication. This porter was once, like C.R., highly esteemed for his wisdom. In fact he had been a famous astrologer. He had, however, committed an act which condemned him to remain as guardian of the gate of the Mysteries. This act, it transpires, is the same that C.R. has committed, of beholding the Lady Venus unveiled. The porter has to remain in this function until he is replaced by whoever next commits this rare and grave act. The supplication asserts that the Lady Venus has again recently been unveiled and the porter now seeks his release.

In the meantime it is announced that, as a reward for their diligence, each one present shall receive as a gift, the thing that he most desires. While they reflect on this the King and Queen play a species of chess where all the pieces represent vices and virtues.

After a final banquet it is announced that they must all take the vows appropriate to being a member of the order of the Knights of the Golden Stone. These are, in brief:

1. That their esoteric order shall be firmly ascribed to the service of God and his hand-maiden, Nature—not to any intervening daimon or spirit.

    (This is important, it is dangerous for an esoteric group or individual to give unquestioning allegiance to a mere discarnate entity.)

2. That they abjure sexual promiscuity, incontinence, or similar deviance.

    (This is particularly important in modern permissive times. The powerful nature of the occult forces can easily spill over into the projection of glamours. The ensuing sexual licence can be corrosive, inflicting great harm to the young by the resultant emotional instability and even destruction of a home. Thus the innocent become disinherited even in their cradles of their fundamental human rights. Esoteric practice, especially in its so-called tantrik forms, demands a strict moral code, not a lack of it.)

3. That they be ready to assist with their talents all who are worthy.

    (The purpose of esoteric training and initiation is service. It is service to others that is its entire justification. However, that service is given to those 'who are worthy'. There are occasions, and many of them, when the service required is not at all what the recipient thinks it should be. That is another angle on the mechanism and motivation of prayer. We should ask for what we need, rather than for what we think we want. The two seldom coincide.)

4. That they do not employ their membership of the Order as a means to worldly pride or authority.

   (The values of the spirit are not those of the world. These strictures not to use the occult arts for gain are very much deeper in implication than a disapproval of commercial clairvoyance. The spiritual principle of love and service is indeed an antithesis to seeking worldly power and glory. There is a spiritual power and glory that shines through those great in love and service, but it is not necessarily coincidental with personal wealth or a position of power or influence.)

5. That they shall not be willing to live longer than God will have them.

   (This seems a strange condition. It is however an acceptance of death, or the conditions of mortality. Initiation is indeed rightly considered a form of death; it is a going forth into the 'shining kingdom' whilst still in the flesh. This is no mere figure of speech.)

These promises are vowed upon the King's sceptre and dedicated in a chapel, where C.R. leaves his hat with the golden tokens, and his golden fleece, and records his name in a book. Above his name he also writes a curious motto: *Summa Scientia Nihil Scire:* 'The highest wisdom is to know nothing'.

This is not merely an injunction to humility. It is an affirmation that intellectual learning is not enough, or indeed even necessary. The 'nothingness' is the spiritual condition above all intuition and intellection. It is beyond what Qabalists call Kether the Crown, the first emanation of God. It is at the heart of the Unmanifest Light known ultimately as AIN—Nothingness. A similar conception is found at the heights of oriental mysticism as the Void, which is beyond the bliss of Nirvana. It is also found in the classic Western treatise on the 'via negativa' *The Cloud of Unknowing.*

Each brother is then granted a private audience with the King and his ministers, to tell what it is he desires above all things. At this point C.R. confesses that it is he who has penetrated to the hiddenmost depths of the mysteries of the castle and seen the naked sleeping Venus. That is, he has done that which no living man can ordinarily do, gaze upon Isis Unveiled—the conscious creative principle behind the manifestations of the natural world.

This is 'naturing Nature'—the active principle of form life (*natura naturans*)—which gives life, variety of form, vitality, evolutionary processes, transformation to 'natured nature', (*natura naturata*). Even simple perception at this level is guarded from mortal man. For were he to be able to go on, and bring influence to bear at this level, then he would be able to control the manifesting forms of life. With an unredeemed will the deed would result in disease, malformation, monsterism, rather than transformation and transmutation to more beautiful and functional life forms. Even so, with scientific tinkering on the outer limits of form, something of the dynamisms involved is revealed in the malformations and malfunctions attendant upon sub-atomic radiations, to say nothing of the genetic engineering implicit in experimentation upon cellular life forms.

The implications of alchemy are thus seen to be grave indeed. It is not merely a matter of mixing and processing various ingredients in order to obtain a precious metal. The ability to transform and transmute the forms of manifesting life would give an horrendous power. Hence the strictures of purity of motive and dedication to the service of God in alchemical texts. These are no mere empty formalities of assumed piety. One may here catch a glimpse of the type of evil that necessitated a whole civilization being wiped off the face of the Earth in volcanic fire, earthquake or deluge, in the tradition of Atlantis. Once the springs of life form are controlled by unregenerate man the types of exploitation, slavery and degradation possible exceed even the vilest abuses of human and animal life performed by man in the current historical epoch.

As a consequence of his attaining this degree of knowledge and power, that is implicit upon his having unveiled the Isis of Nature, C.R. is told by Atlas that he may not now return home. He must take the place of the old porter as guardian of the castle gate. Furthermore, no release can be expected until another penetrates the same Mystery, and this will not be until the next

Chymical Marriage, in a new generation, of the current King/Bridegroom's future son.

C.R. now realizes why he was so warmly welcomed by the porter initially, who indeed said, 'Now welcome in God's Name unto me the man whom of long time I would gladly have seen'. This describes a particular function of esoteric grade or office: that one so privileged has to train his successor before he may pass on himself.

This particular office is custodian of the Rosicrucian Mysteries. It is a high one, as is implied by the long wait that is envisaged before another may be found sufficiently worthy. In the higher grades of the Planetary Hierarchy this may entail a period longer than the normal human life span. C.R. is also evidently of an equal grade to the Lord of the Tower and even Atlas, with both of whom he shares a glorious lodging.

Here the manuscript abruptly breaks off on the pretext that the last two leaves of it are missing. However this is a device that conceals the fact that the three remain sleeping, like the uncorrupted body of Christian Rosencreutz, or the Lady Venus, or heroes such as King Arthur of Avalon, or Merlin of the hawthorn tower of Nimue, until such time as they are awakened by one who is found worthy. Then the remaining pages of the manuscript will be written in terms of the life experiences of the one who performs the awakening.

Part Four:
The Mysteries of Isis

We have spent much time considering the detailed imagery of a seventeenth-century interpretation of the Mysteries of the Goddess. They indeed are the mysteries of the Rose in the Rose Cross. The feminine powers have a prominent place within it—the Virgin of Lights and all her maidens, the Queen whose altar it is that contains the seven central Mysteries, the sleeping Lady Venus, the active Cupid who is the child of the goddess of love. All are clear indications of the feminine power and the creative sexual dynamics or kundalini that is at the centre of the Mysteries. We will now examine an example of these self-same Mysteries from a different period, as revealed in 'The Transformations of Lucius Apuleius of Madura', popularly called *The Golden Ass*. This was written in the second century AD, one and a half millenia prior to *The Chymical Marriage*. Lucius Apuleius, born c. 120 AD, was an initiate in the Mysteries of Isis, and his book is more revealing of the Mysteries of Isis than most people suspect.

The original is written in a high flown form of Latin prose, the nearest modern equivalent of which might be 'stage Irish'. Apuleius' other works, a Discourse on Magic, and an exposition on the Daimon of Socrates, were written in clear straightforward Latin. *The Golden Ass* is a parody of a professional story-teller's style of the times. Robert Graves suggests that the catchphrase of these gentlemen: 'Give me a copper coin and I'll tell you a golden story', is in part responsible for the more popular title of Golden Ass. This may be so but we would also suggest that there is an alchemical tinge to this gold. That it is indicative of pure and priceless Mysteries concealed beneath the surface of the tale.

Just as the wisdom of the Tarot was preserved because it was put in the form of a common card game, so with the Golden Ass. It is at base simply an elaboration of an ancient Greek dirty joke and has come down the ages as a comic erotic novel. Human nature being as it is we find that the complete texts of Apuleius' other books have not survived, and are rare volumes in the libraries of academe, whereas the Golden Ass has not only survived, but is freely available in cheap paper-back form to this day.

There are many hints that this is no ordinary comic story. In his preface, Lucius Apuleius 'apologises' for the rustic Egyptian overtones of his animal-god story. Yet those readers of his own times would know this to be a broad hint about hidden meanings. Egypt was at that time a legendary treasure-house of ancient mysteries and magical powers.

He also traces a family lineage for himself, claiming ancestors who lived on Mount Hymettus, near Athens, (famous for its honey, a substance particularly symbolic of the mystery religions) and at Taenarus in Laconia (which is the traditional site of the entrance to Hades). The Golden Ass is therefore a form of literature known in later Rosicrucian days as a 'ludibrium', a fantastic tale embodying great truths, of which another example is *The Chymical Marriage of Christian Rosencreutz*.

The disadvantage of this type of literature is that it can easily be misunderstood, and Apuleius' book is particularly prone to this. More prudish editions of the past have tended to leave bits out, with discreet lines of dots where the plot becomes too vulgar. On the other hand, and perhaps more indicative of our own times, there are versions which leave in the vulgarity and cut out the religious parts. This narrowness of vision is also to be found in the academic world. Some scholars feel that the hand that wrote some of the more earthy adventures of the ass could not possibly have written the beautiful spiritual visions of other parts. Thus do the blind try to deny sight to those who can see. Apuleius is no pornographer who has had his work tampered with by a spiritual hand, for whatever peculiar motive. He is a profoundly wise initiate who is able to regard life as it is, from the spiritual heights to the most depraved depths, and to forge a message of hope and instruction from it all.

In his story, if one reads between the lines, is a very full exposition of the realities of initiation into the Mysteries. To those who have trod a few steps along the Way the experiences described by Apuleius have a familiar ring. This is the Ariadne's thread we may use through the labyrinth of the asses' adventures; for recognition of living experience may prove a surer guide than the erudition of the classical scholar.

The basis of Apuleius' tale is an ancient Greek ribald joke about a man who was changed into an ass by witchcraft, and found that in this guise he was loved by a woman of unusual sexual appetite. Later he manages to change back into human form and eagerly presents himself to his lover, only to find that she spurns him, preferring him in his assinine form because of the superior sexual endowment of an ass.

It is upon this unpromising foundation that Apuleius built a profound story of initiation into the Mysteries of Isis. When Lucius, the hero of the story, is turned into an ass he falls into a semi-animal condition from a higher state of being. This is analogous to the Neo-Platonic idea of the human spirit falling into material existence, the word of the flesh. The subsequent adventures of the ass are thus parallel to the initiations of the Mysteries, that lead from the material world to the condition of the unfallen spirit.

At the start of his adventures Lucius is a very high minded young man, filled with the noblest of intentions, and complete even with a white charger in best ideal romantic knightly tradition. In a sense his condition is similar to the innocent Fool of the Tarot. It is also significant that he is going to visit the country of his mother, for Isis is the mother of us all, of all nature.

In her interpretation of the story, Marie Louise von Franz (*The Golden Ass of Apuleius—A Psychological Interpretation*), a Jungian psychologist, regards this and much that is to follow in terms of a man with a positive mother complex delineating a case study of a negative mother complex. This kind of interpretation may be helpful to psychotherapists but is a somewhat limited view of the great dual Mysteries of the Black Isis and the White Isis. There may well be useful parallels to be drawn between analytical psychology and magic, one with its approach to the Unconscious, the other to the Anima Mundi or the Astral Light, but such terms are not necessarily completely interchangeable. We must beware of substituting one set of ill-understood and inadequate terms for another set of ill-understood and inadequate terms and thinking that we are gaining great wisdom thereby.

In the early stages of the story Lucius receives three warnings. In effect these charge him to ensure that his motives are correct. This is in accordance with the prime injunction of all Mystery training.

The first warning is a story from a cheese and honey merchant whom he meets on the way. Both products that this merchant, Aristomenes, sells have close associations with the Mysteries, and particularly those of the Great Mother, in the Dionysian, Eleusinian and Orphic rites.

Aristomenes' story is what we would nowadays call a black comedy. It tells of his efforts to rescue an intellectual old miser, named Socrates, from the toils of a witch, Meroë, who has seduced him and holds him in bondage. The use of the name Socrates is no coincidence, for however great the wisdom of the original Socrates may have been, he came to be the caricature, in the popular mind, for the logic chopping intellectualized pedant. One who has cut himself off from his emotional and instinctual roots and is prey to a sudden uprush from them.

In spite of Aristomenes' efforts Meroë and her accomplice catch up with Socrates and, through a wound in his throat, steal his heart. The Daath/Yesod and Tiphareth significance of this will be plain to any Qabalist. The warning to the idealistic young Lucius is not to become too preoccupied with the 'higher' things, for the lower have an unexpected and unfortunate way of taking their revenge for being so discounted, betrayed and neglected.

Lucius proceeds to the nearby town and takes lodgings at a household which has a close resemblance to Aristomenes' story. It belongs to an old bore and miser, named Milos, who is married to a seductive witch called Pamphile.

Also in the household is an attractive young slave girl called Fotis, on whose actions much of the adventures that befall Lucius depend. She is, in effect, the Opener of the Ways for him. Her name is in fact derived from the Greek word for light, just as the name Lucius is derived from the Roman word for light. This is another indication that we are concerned with a story of illumination.

Lucius, on his arrival at the town, is full of all the naïve and superstitious speculations that beset the new student of the Mysteries. In this overheated mood he wanders into the provision market to buy some fish. Here he meets an old student friend and the subsequent exchange with him is typical of relationships between tyros in the early stages of seeking esoteric wisdom. His friend gazes at the fish he has bought, condemns it as worthless, berates the fishmonger from whom it was purchased, and in righteous moral indignation throws the fish on the ground and stamps it into paste. Thereupon he goes off congratulating himself on helping a friend and upon his own moral rectitude. As a result poor Lucius is left supperless. Thus do many newcomers to the Mysteries wantonly criticize the beliefs and institutions of their contemporaries, without being able to replace the faith that they destroy with anything better.

In the same market Lucius has a more productive encounter, with Byrrhaenea, a foster-sister and cousin of his mother's, and who had nursed him when he was young. She is thus a surrogate for the goddess, and in this role gives him his second warning. This she does by inviting him to her house where there is displayed an impressive group of statues. They show the virgin huntress goddess Diana about to bathe, with the face of Actaeon peering through the bushes at her, already half transformed into a stag; after which he was torn to pieces by his own hounds as punishment for seeking to gaze upon the unveiled goddess. This is a warning to Lucius to look to his purity of motive. However, as so often happens, the warning serves only to inflame his curiosity, and he hurries off with irresistible urge to study the dark magic of his hostess Pamphile.

What in fact immediately transpires is the mutual seduction of Lucius and Fotis. This commences in the kitchen; and, throughout this story, food and the place where it is prepared, occur again and again. They signify spiritual nourishment, the food of the Mysteries. There is also more implied in the union of Lucius and Fotis than the assuaging of sexual appetite, for there is a sustained analogy throughout of the conjunction of Venus and Mars.

Roses also feature largely in this scene. Fotis comes to Lucius' bed bearing wine and roses. The wine she sups like a dove (a bird sacred to Venus), and the roses (also sacred to Venus) she strews on and around the bed. She has a rose between her breasts and puts a chaplet of roses about Lucius' head.

Following this event Lucius receives his third and final warning. This is at a party held by Byrrhaenea and is a story told by Thelyphron, a fellow guest. He has been badly mutilated about the face through becoming involved with witchcraft and sorcery in a sceptical fashion, and indeed he would have fared much worse but for the intervention of an Egyptian priest. This emphasizes the connection of the story with the Mysteries of Isis and Osiris, wherein the body of Osiris is mutilated by Set and restored by Isis.

Following hard upon this final warning Lucius finds himself the subject of a ritual of initiation—although he does not realize this at the time. He returns late to his house where he sees three villains trying to storm the gate. He thereupon attacks and kills them. A doorway is, of course, of initiatory significance, and the three villains have a parallel to those to be met in the Hiram legend of Freemasonry.

The next day he finds himself accused of murder and is dragged to court with a great crowd in attendance. So great is the crowd that the case has to be transferred to a theatre—which is another suggestion that we have a ritual drama. Here he undergoes trial, and is berated by a mourning mother, and a wife and child of the murdered men. As a final preliminary to being sentenced, tortured and put to death he is ordered, as a salutary humiliation, to withdraw the cloths that cover the bodies of his victims. Much against his will, he is pressed to do so, only to find that instead of human corpses they are inflated wine skins. The whole assembly breaks into laughter and it is revealed that he has taken part in a festival of Risus, the god of laughter.

Whether or not a public joke, this has been a profound initiation for him. As Dostoevsky pointed out, who was once similarly condemned to death and reprieved at the last minute, after such an experience one is never quite the same again. Lucius has entered, through this initiatory drama, the porchway entrance of the gates of death—and as an innocent victim. This has profound parallels in pagan and Christian theology. The wine skins suggest the Dionysiac Mysteries, references to which occur throughout the story.

An initiation ceremony often presages or confirms actual events, or stages of realization, in daily life. Following upon this one Lucius has the choice of taking up or refusing the adverse side of magical operation. Pamphile is in the midst of great conjurations and Lucius and Fotis plan to spy on her. Following upon this resolution of deceit and overweening curiosity it is not insignificant that their sexual relationship takes a twisted turn, first 'In Bacchic fury' and then 'as though she were a boy'. Expressions of outer and inner life go hand in hand.

Soon after they see Pamphile rub ointment upon herself and turn into an owl, whereupon she flies off into the night. Lucius is determined to emulate this act, which, as a flying soul, might be likened to etheric or astral projections. He prevails upon Fotis to steal some of the ointment. However, in keeping with the atmosphere of intrigue and betrayal, they choose the wrong box, and instead of turning into an owl (a creature sacred to Persephone and Pallas Athene and associated with wisdom) he turns into the Set-like beast most abhorred by Isis—an ass.

Not only this, before any counter-potion can be taken (which is the apparently simple expedient of eating roses) their own act of theft takes on an objective reality. Thieves break into the house, steal all the valuables therein, and kidnap the ass to carry off the loot.

At the bandits' hide-out we find the elements for another Mystery drama. There is a young bride called Charitë, who has been seized and carried off on her wedding day by the bandits. Typical of the god/goddess relationship of ancient Egypt (e.g., Isis and Osiris) she and her bridegroom Tlepolemus are also cousins and have slept together since infancy.

To console the desolate and weeping bride an old crone who lives with the robbers tells the story of Cupid and Psyche. This is perhaps the most spiritually inspired tale of pagan antiquity to portray the condition of the human soul.

Psyche is one of three royal daughters, and so beautiful that many take her to be the incarnation of a goddess. This is also her misfortune for, whilst her plainer sisters are successfully married, Psyche is so adored that she has no normal human contact. All who see her seek to place her on a pedestal. This excites the wrath of the goddess Venus whose shrines are being neglected. As a lesson Venus instructs her son Cupid to cause Psyche to fall in love with some degraded outcast. By a neat ironical twist the 'degraded outcast' turns out to be Cupid himself.

In the meantime Psyche's father seeks advice at the oracle of Apollo and receives the prophecy that she shall be wed on a mountain top, and not to a human but to a feared and mischievous winged terror. In fact the mountain top may be conceived as the heights of human mystical aspiration, and the 'winged terror' is Cupid himself, the embodiment of divine love. Taking the prophecy in its literal sense, with much grief Psyche is taken to a mountain top and left there to her fate.

A gentle West wind however wafts her to a beautiful land where, in an enchanted castle, she is tended by invisible servants ministering to her every wish. And when night falls she is taken in marriage by an invisible husband. He is in fact Cupid himself who tells her that she must never seek to gaze upon him. This, in a sense, is a polar opposite to the dilemma of Christian Rosencreutz and the Lady Venus.

So life goes idyllically on in this paradisal condition but Psyche conceives an ever stronger desire to see her sisters and to show them her circumstances of life. She is counselled against this by Cupid but in the end he lets her have her way. Her sisters come to visit but are consumed by jealousy and rabidly curious as to who her secret husband might be.

When they return home they hide the gifts of jewels they have been given and say nothing about the visit to their mourning parents, who still grieve the apparent cruel fate of Psyche.

When Psyche wishes to see her sisters again Cupid once more warns her about the dangers that might ensue, particularly as she is now with child by him. She can see no danger however and persists in her desire that her sisters come again. When they do so they tell her that they are much concerned for her, that they have discovered she is in fact married to a hideous evil monster. They advise her to hide a lamp and a knife near her bed and when her husband next comes to her in the night to raise the lamp and cut his head off with the knife.

Deceived by their wiles Psyche does as they suggest, but when she raises the lamp to strike with the knife she is struck helpless by the beauty of the naked god. Even the blade of the knife turns at the vision, and a spot of hot oil from the lamp awakens Cupid. For her betrayal and disobedience Cupid rebukes her and vows the evil sisters shall have their just desserts. As for Psyche, her punishment shall simply be—the cruellest that a God of Love can inflict—his absence.

Desolate in her fallen condition Psyche meets Pan, the most earthy representative of the power of love. He advises her not to despair but simply to have the faith and loyalty to go on loving the God of Love, as this is the only way that he can be invoked to reappear. She returns to her own country.

One of her sisters, on learning that Psyche's husband was in fact a god, mad with envious desire, runs up to the mountain top and casts herself off. But no gentle sustaining West wind comes and she crashes to her death on the rocks, which cut her to pieces, and the birds and beasts of the mountain consume her remains.

Psyche finds herself an outcast. She is turned away from the temples of Ceres and Juno, who tell her that her only hope is to reconcile herself with Venus. Venus however is enraged at Cupid's disobedience of her original edict and at his mating with a mortal. When Psyche approaches, the goddess Venus has her scourged by two servants, Anxiety and Grief, and in mockery gives her a series of impossible tests as the only means to re-instate herself.

These are:

   (i) to sort a huge pile of seeds in a single night;
  (ii) to collect a skein of golden fleece from a flock of ferocious rams;
 (iii) to fill a cup with water from the high spring that feeds the Styx, the river dividing this world from the Underworld;
  (iv) to descend into Hades and return with a box containing some of the beauty of Proserpine.

Psyche, however, succeeds in performing these tasks, with the help of others. The ants, emblematic of industry and civilization, sort the seeds for her. The simple wisdom of the riverside reeds advises her to collect the fleece from briars while the rams are asleep. The eagle, who was helped by Cupid to raise the cup-bearer Ganymede to heaven at Zeus' command, returns the favour by procuring the cupful of water for Psyche. To perform the final test Psyche ascends a tower with the intention of throwing herself from the top to her death. The tower, however, tells her that although this is a way to reach the Underworld it is a way that precludes her returning. The wise tower (obviously a structure of initiation) gives her detailed advice on how to enter the Underworld, find her way through its passages and tests to Proserpine, and how safely to return. Psyche follows this advice and returns with the box of Proserpine's beauty. Even here she almost fails, when her human curiosity gets the better of her. She tries to peep at the beauty inside the box but on opening it is overcome with sleep. Cupid, however, comes to her aid, and all ends happily. Zeus regularizes their marriage and makes Psyche immortal.

So ends the story told by the hag (another form of the goddess) to the captive Charitë. Like Psyche, Charitë seeks the help of lower creatures and begs help from the ass. He, although he is lame (a parallel with the lameness of Oedipus and the supreme lame god, Asclepios) gallops off with her on his back—beauty and the beast. In this scene is embodied the relationship between Higher Self and Lower Self as taught in esoteric psychology. As so often happens, rider and ridden have a difference of opinion as to which way to go. Charitë wants to ride straight home; Lucius the ass knows that this is the way the robbers have gone. They are still disputing at the parting of the ways when the robbers return and recapture them.

Further rescue comes in a most unexpected way. The robbers elect a new chief who seems to be a very superior kind of robber. In fact it is Charitë's bridegroom in disguise. He overcomes the robbers, delivers them to justice, and marries his bride. Thus we have the drama of a saviour god coming among men to restore things to rights.

For his attempt to save Charitë, the ass is rewarded in a fashion thought most likely to please an ass. He is sent to a stud farm. However, all does not go well for him at the stud farm. His further adventures parallel the Mystery drama that has been enacted by Charitë (the stolen and ransomed virgin bride) and Tlepolemus (the saviour bridegroom descending to a lower condition to effect her rescue and redemption).

The couple do not live happily ever after. Tlepolemus is

betrayed by a former rival for her hand. He is invited on a
hunting expedition, and although he has vowed never to hunt
horned or tusked beasts (sacred to Isis), things are so arranged
that he is cornered and gored by a ferocious boar. The rival,
Thrasyllus, finishes him off and then, feigning innocence,
proceeds to woo the widowed Charitë.

She, however, is informed of the facts by the ghost of her
murdered husband. She pretends to welcome the murderer's
advances, and even to agree to a secret love affair before their
marriage. However, on the night that she promised to come to
his bed she drugs him and blinds him with a bronze pin from her
hair. She then flies to her husband's grave and kills herself with
his sword, plunging it under the right breast—where Jesus also
received the lance thrust from Longinus.

There are interesting parallels in all of this story with
Christian and pagan mysteries, and also with some of
Shakespeare's plots. Of particular significance is that on her
husband's grave Charitë erects an image of the god Dionysius,
endowed with her husband's features. Tlepolemus, a saviour
like Dionysius, is torn by a wild beast as Dionysius was by the
Bacchanals. This death of the saviour is occasioned by a rival
whose name means 'rashness', or the impiety that comes from
presumption and envy. This gives the opportunity for a noble,
martyr's death, in a love that transcends the grave, for Charitë,
whose name signifies hope and love. This episode shows the
close parallels that lie between certain pagan Mystery cults and
the Christian interpretation of the significance of Jesus, who is
an historical embodiment of pagan spiritual insights as much as
a fulfilment of the Old Testament Jewish prophetic tradition.

In parallel to these events, the asses' stay at the stud farm is
not a happy one. First he is shunned and persecuted by the
horses, who look down upon him as inferior to themselves. And
in defiance of express orders for his honourable treatment, the
steward's evil wife sets him to work slaving at a mill. He is also
cruelly overworked and tortured by a sadistic boy. The theme of
evil wife and mill-turning appear more than once in the
narrative. The evil wife is the averse side of womanhood, and a
distorted aspect of Isis, invoked by Lucius' underhand means
and motives in his approach to her Mysteries.

The mill is an interesting symbol in that it is a symbol of

harnessed power. It can be beneficent in its technological results or a form of slavery. The symbol of the swastika derives from it, being the plan view of a mill spindle driven by four beasts via transverse poles.

Just as the evil wife, the nagging shrew, is the averse side of the goddess; so the sadistic boy is the averse side of the divine miraculous child. Poor Lucius certainly reaps as he has sown in his impious approach to the Mysteries.

This is the nadir of his treatment. Having been well punished by the circumstances evoked by his own attitude (the true operation of karma) his sufferings are brought to an end by a she-bear killing the sadistic boy. The she-bear is another emblem of the goddess Isis, and signifies her intervention. This is in the nick of time for, as a result of the boy's falsely accusing him of trying to molest little girls, plans were afoot to castrate the ass. Even so, he suffers a cruel beating from the boy's avenging mother, who blames him for her son's death.

We may consider this episode as a period of purgation. It is an established step in any initiation process, and precedes the next stage of initiation, which is a desert or wilderness journey.

This journey is brought about, in the story, by the steward and his wife deciding to abscond with all the goods and chattels on hearing of the death of Tlepolemus and Charitë. Thus Lucius finds himself once again in the hands of thieves, but with the slight improvement that these are amateur rather than professional thieves.

The initiatory character of the wilderness journey (in this instance, through a forest) is shown by its having three crisis points within it. The first is their fear that they will be attacked by wolves. In fact they are attacked by the mastiff dogs of the village where they seek refuge. The villagers also throw stones at them in the belief that they are bandits. There are two interesting aspects to this. First the principle that what one fears does not generally happen in the way that one expects. Secondly that although they are not bandits, as the villagers fear, they are certainly thieves, and thus not undeserving of the treatment they receive. So divine justice (or karma) acts through ordinary levels of causation in a seemingly arbitrary but, at root, just fashion.

The second crisis is where they are duped by an old man who allegedly seeks help to rescue a child. In fact he is custodian of a dreadful snake monster who lures unwary travellers to their death. Again this reflects themselves as betrayers of trust.

The third crisis is their confrontation with the fate of a false bailiff (as they themselves are), who because he betrayed his wife and child (a particular sin against Isis) is sentenced to be tied to a fig tree smeared with honey where he is eaten alive by ants. The ants we have met before in the story of Cupid and Psyche; and figs and honey are both sacred to the Mysteries of the Goddess.

In the normal sequence of events, after the Mystery journey through the Wilderness, the candidate for initiation would come upon a temple. We are enacting, however, in the story of Lucius, a distorted shadow of the true Mysteries. This is partly to warn of the consequences of their desecration; partly as a convenient 'blind' for Apuleius not to reveal too much to the 'profane'. Consequently we have a distorted portrayal of an initiate's reception into a band of devoted brothers. Lucius, the ass, finds himself purchased by a wandering group of holy men. These are described as Eunuch-priests (as indeed many priests of the Goddess were) but in fact they are homosexuals of a most predatory kind, who make their living by performing ecstatic dances of self-flagellation and collecting money from the impressed onlookers. They require the ass to carry a statue of the Eastern goddess Cybele, whose adherents they purport to be.

Lucius describes his falling into their hands as the work of 'merciless Fortune' which is what the ancient classical world would have called karma. A changed attitude can bring about a changed circumstance so, at root, any 'lack of mercy' is a lack of repentance.

A couple of interesting points are made in the text about pseudo-religious experience and pseudo-occult knowledge. The first is in his description of pretended ecstacy of one of the priests—'heaving deep sighs from the very bottom of his lungs, as if filled with the spirit of the Goddess, he pretended to go stark-mad'. He goes on to comment: 'A strange notion, this, that divine immanency, instead of doing men good, enfeebles or disorders their senses'. The other amusing point, which might well be applied by occult charlatans of today, is their all-purpose oracle. To any who come seeking prophetic guidance they chant:

The patient oxen plough the soil;
And harvests rich repay their toil.

This can be applied to any conceivable problem as a welcome generally optimistically-toned allusive answer from the gods.

The ass remains with the eunuch priests for some time, carrying the image of the goddess and the ever full offertory bags. 'I was at once a walking temple and a walking larder' he says, again emphasizing the recurrent symbolism throughout the whole novel of the sacramental symbolism of eating and feasting. This again is universal symbolism found from the ever flowing Cauldron of Ceridwen to the table of the Last Supper.

While he is with them he faces the first of three tests of moral integrity. At some risk to himself he raises the alarm when the eunuch priests attempt to rape a young farm worker. Thus although an ass he shows more than an asses' concern for the well-being of others.

Later he exposes the deception that a cook intends to play in serving up ass' meat instead of venison, although there is a certain degree of self-interest here in that it is he who is likely to provide the ass meat if the cook's scheme goes through. There is an overtone here of the saviour god theme, the hero being eaten. However there are more immediate spiritual developments required of Lucius as he is eventually to become an initiate of the Mysteries to which his experiences in animal form are a prelude. The test here is one of super-assinine intelligence in that he saves himself by smashing up the dining room and then sheltering in the Master's bedroom, where he spends the night. There is another interesting piece of symbolism here in the role of the dog. Anubis, the Egyptian Opener of the Ways, is a dog-headed god, and the ways are opened in this episode first by a dog stealing the haunch of venison (which is the circumstance that leads the cook to kill and serve up the ass), and then he is left unmolested in the bedroom because another dog is found to be rabid and so all fear to go near the ass in case he too has rabies, his actions in smashing up the dining room being thought the symptoms of the disease.

Following this episode the eunuch priests are arrested for having stolen a golden cup from the temple of Juno. This is an apt symbolic statement of sin against the feminine principle which is the inner side of their homosexual proclivities. The ass is sold again, once more coming under the dominion of an evil and adulterous wife at a mill, and the ass' third moral act is to expose her deception of her husband by revealing her lover.

An interesting historical side-light here is that the woman appears to be a Christian, and in the author's words: 'She ... professed perfect scorn for the immortals and rejected all true religion in favour of a fantastic and blasphemous cult of an "Only God". In his honour she practised various absurd ceremonies which gave her the excuse of getting drunk quite early in the day and playing the whore at all hours; most people, including her husband, were quite deceived by her.'

Plainly Apuleius has no great love of Christians and this early example of relations between the new religion and the old is an interesting one. If this travesty of early Christian belief and practice was the common attitude of intelligent pagans then there is small wonder that when Christians came to power they took such unsympathetic views of paganism.

The time scale is also worth note. Apuleius was writing in about AD 160, and although he was an intelligent and spiritually informed initiate, he had obviously only a minor and passing acquaintance with the religion that was to dominate the West in the next two thousand years. He is writing 130 years after the crucifixion of Jesus, and about two hundred years before the new religion would officially replace paganism. Putting this into a modern context, if we were to assume that Apuleius were writing now, the crucifixion of Jesus would have taken place in 1849, his birth in 1819, and his religion would not become officially embraced until the end of the twenty-third century! Those who expect the imminent appearance of the Aquarian Age might do well to reflect upon this time scale. If, as many think, a new avatar might have been born in the remarkable conjunction of planets in 1962, unless things move very much faster in the changing of human hearts and ideas, no radical acceptance of his coming is likely until about 2300!

Following the successful completion of these tests of moral initiative (akin to the parable of the Good Samaritan, which many humans have yet to learn), Lucius is relieved by a more fortunate interlude when he passes into the hands of a market gardener, helping him to take his food to market—another instance of spiritual food symbolism.

This does not last however. It is a phase quickly followed by what is called in the mystical terminology of St John of the Cross, 'the dark night of the soul', or in terms of alchemy, the *dissolutio.* Everything falls to pieces.

There are, first of all, a series of frightening portents. The ancient world took portents seriously. In the histories of Livy, for instance, along with the historical details of the year's events, the major portents or omens are also listed. The modern mind tends to sneer at this preoccupation, but as Jung has found and reported in his work on synchronicity, when one approaches the inner worlds particularly, whether in analytical psychology, Mystery initiation, or the psychic upsurge caused by great national events, signs preceding (or portents) and signs following are to be expected. Admittedly, interpreting them may be difficult, but the inner worlds have a way of making their presence felt in no uncertain manner. They are, after all, levels of causation, even though the effects of that causation work out in a perfectly ordinary 'accustomed' way.

The strange portents are swiftly followed by bad news, of corruption and death, and following upon this the most unlikely things happen. The most significant of which is the old market gardener turning upon a centurion who tries to commandeer the ass and beating him up and leaving him unconscious. They then become fugitives, for assaulting a Roman army officer is a serious offence, and they go into hiding. Their hiding place is betrayed however by the asses' shadow showing up against a wall. Thus are we all betrayed by our 'shadow' side. It is that which constitutes the Dweller on the Threshold of Initiation and causes all the life problems that we have, as our own averse side is projected onto the world about us.

These unfortunate occurrences are however the prelude to initiation and are at least a sign that progress is being made. From now on Lucius is on a plainly discernible upward path that leads first to his leaving behind his assinine form, and then his higher initiation into the rites of Isis and Osiris.

We need to bear in mind however, if we are to avoid the pitfall of vainglory and ego-inflation, that although it behoves us to try our best, it is not by our own merits alone that we achieve initiation. We need help from others, and we need Divine Grace. This is signified by the story that is interpolated here of an innocent victim only being saved from evil machinations by the intervention of a *deus ex machina* in the form of a holy medical man.

Having got his attitude right through the numerous tests, realizations and retributions that have gone before, Lucius is set for initiation, the stages of which follow in the narrative, beginning from the point where he is put into kitchen service (again the symbolism of spiritual food) with the Lord Chief Justice. This symbolizes law, order and the civilizing process represented by initiation and the aims and aspirations of the Masters of the Wisdom. More than one of the Masters of the Wisdom has been a Lord Chief Justice, or Lord Chancellor, in his time.

From the time that Lucius in his assinine form is taken into service by the Lord Chief Justice his development shows rapid progress. Working as a pack animal attached to the kitchen he begins to leave his hay and to feed on human food left over from the banquets.

He is discovered in this, but his masters, far from punishing him, encourage him to do more human tricks. They teach him to sit at table, to wrestle, to dance, to nod or shake his head in answer to questions, and even to wink at the wine waiter when he needs a drink. He soon becomes quite famous as a result.

We have in this episode an analogue of spiritual initiation. Just as the ass is being trained to become more human, prior to resuming his original and proper human form, from which state he has fallen; so in the initiation process is the human personality trained into more spiritual attitudes and patterns prior to regaining its original and proper spiritual condition from which it has fallen.

In *The Golden Ass* this process reaches its peak in the visit of a noblewoman who takes the ass and trains it to be her lover. Keeping in mind the consistent symbolic parallels we see how Apuleius has transformed the original dirty joke into an initiatory parable, for this represents the human soul being taken into close consummation with the goddess—the higher realms of inner nature—or Isis Unveiled.

However, just as the highest mysteries are capable of the

greatest profanation, so in the story do we get a degrading of the situation. The relationship between the noblewoman and the ass is treated by Apuleius with considerable literary skill and good taste. It is a genuine love that is depicted, which reminds one of the delicacy of the feelings of Titania the Fairy Queen for Bottom, the Ass-headed, in Shakespeare's *Midsummer Night's Dream*. In the story word gets out, and it is decided that it would be amusing and profitable to make a public spectacle of this new feat of the ass.

This kind of divertissement occurred frequently in Roman times. Scenes from mythology were used as the material for public spectacle. In this instance the show is to be the Judgment of Paris, which provides an excuse for a display of feminine nudity. And as a sequel to this, a condemned criminal woman is to be coupled with the ass, before she is torn to pieces by wild beasts.

However, the ass has by now achieved a measure of sensibility and morality superior to his human owners, and rather than take part in such public profanation of the Mysteries, he runs away—renouncing a life of assinine ease, fame and fortune.

He runs to the sea-shore and there makes a sincere and passionate supplication to the goddess Isis to save him and restore him to his rightful form. This, his invocation and the subsequent appearance to him of the goddess, is possibly the most moving and evocative passage in ancient literature. To the occult student it is the very stuff of 'path-working' and similar meditational image building. Some may, at some time, be fortunate enough to experience such a vision themselves.

About the first watch of the night, when as I had slept my first sleep, I awaked with sudden fear, and saw the moon shining bright as when she is at the full, and seeming as though she leaped out of the sea. Then I thought with myself that this was the most secret time, when that goddess had most puissance and force, considering that all human things be governed by her providence; and that not only all beasts private and tame, wild and savage, be made strong by the governance of her light and godhead, but also things inanimate and without life: and I considered that all bodies in the heavens, the earth, and the seas be by her increasing motions increased, and by her diminishing motions diminished; then as weary of all my cruel fortune and calamity, I found good hope and sovereign remedy, though it were very late, to be delivered of all my misery, by invocation and prayer to the excellent beauty of this powerful goddess. Wherefore shaking off my drowsy sleep I arose with a joyful face, and moved by a great affection to purify myself, I plunged my head seven times into the water of the sea; which number of seven is convenable and agreeable to holy and divine things, as the worthy and sage philosopher Pythagoras hath declared. Then very lively and joyfully, though with a weeping countenance, I made this oration to the puissant goddess:

'O blessed queen of heaven, whether Thou be the Dame Ceres which art the original and motherly nurse of all fruitful things in the earth, who, after the finding of thy daughter Proserpine, through the great joy which Thou didst presently conceive, didst utterly take away and abolish the food of them of old time, the acorns, and madest the barren and unfruitful ground of Eleusis to be ploughed and sewn, and now givest men a more better and milder food; or whether Thou be the celestial Venus, who, in the beginning of the world, didst couple together male and female with an engendered love, and didst so make an eternal propagation of human kind, being now worshipped within the temples of the Isle Paphos; or whether Thou be the sister of the god Phoebus, who hast saved so many people by lightening and lessening with thy medicines the pangs of travail and art now adored at the sacred places of Ephesus; or whether Thou be called terrible Proserpine, by reason of the deadly howlings which Thou yieldest, that hath power with triple face to stop and put away the invasion of hags and ghosts which appear unto men, and to keep them down in the closures of the Earth, which dost wander in sundry groves and art worshipped in divers manners; Thou, which dost luminate all the cities of the earth by Thy feminine light; Thou, which nourishest all the seeds of the world by Thy damp heat, giving Thy changing light according to the wanderings, near or far, of the sun: by whatsoever name or fashion or shape it is lawful to call upon Thee, I pray Thee to end my great travail and misery and raise up my fallen hopes, and deliver me from the wretched fortune which so long time pursued me. Grant peace and rest, if it please Thee, to my adversities, for I have endured enough labour and peril. Remove from me the hateful shape of mine ass, and render me to my kindred and to mine own self Lucius: and if I have offended in any point Thy divine majesty, let me rather die if I may not live.'

When I had ended this oration, discovering my plaints to the goddess, I fortuned to fall again asleep upon that same bed; and by and by (for mine eyes were but newly closed) appeared to me from the midst of the sea a divine and venerable face, worshipped even of the gods themselves. Then, by little and little, I seemed to see the whole figure of her body, bright and mounting out of the sea and standing before me: wherefore I purpose to describe her divine semblance, if the poverty of my human speech will suffer me, or her divine power give me a power of eloquence rich enough to express it. First she had a great abundance of hair, flowing and curling, dispersed and scattered about her divine neck; on the crown of her head she bare many garlands interlaced with flowers, and in the middle of her forehead was a plain circlet in fashion of a mirror, or rather resembling the moon by the light that it gave forth; and this was borne up on either side by serpents that seemed to rise from the furrows of the earth, and above it were blades of corn set out. Her vestment was of finest linen yielding divers colours, somewhere white and shining, somewhere yellow like the crocus flower, somewhere rosy red, somewhere flaming; and (which troubled my sight and spirit sore) her cloak was utterly dark and obscure covered with shining black, and being wrapped round her from under her left arm to her right shoulder in manner of a shield, part of it fell down, pleated in most subtle fashion, to the skirts of her garment so that the welts appeared comely. Here and there upon the edge thereof and throughout its surface the stars glimpsed, and in the middle of them was placed the moon in mid-month, which shone like a flame of fire; and round about the whole length of the border of that goodly robe was a crown of garland wreathing unbroken, made with all flowers and all fruits. Things quite diverse did she bear: for in her right hand she had timbrel of brass, a flat piece of metal curved in manner of a girdle, wherein passed not many rods through the periphery of it; and when with her arm she moved these triple chords, they gave forth a shrill and clear sound. In her hand she bare a cup of gold like unto a boat, upon the handle whereof, in the upper part which is best seen, an asp lifted up his head with a wide-swelling throat. Her odoriferous feet were covered with shoes interlaced and wrought with victorious palm. Thus the divine shape, breathing out the pleasant spice of fertile Arabia, disdained not with her holy voice to utter these words unto me:

'Behold Lucius, I am come; thy weeping and prayer hath moved me to succour thee. I am she that is the natural mother of all things, mistress and governess of all the elements, the initial progeny of worlds, chief of the powers divine, queen of all that are in hell, the principal of them that dwell in heaven, manifested alone and under one form of all the gods and goddesses. At my will the planets of the sky, the wholesome winds of the seas, and the lamentable silences of hell be disposed; my name, my divinity is adored throughout all the world, in divers manners, in variable customs, and by many names. For the Phrygians that are the first of all men call me the Mother of the gods at Pessinus; the Athenians, which are sprung from their own soil, Cecropian Minerva; the Cyprians, which are girt about by the sea, Paphian Venus; the Cretans which bear arrows, Dictynnian Diana; the Sicilians, which speak three tongues, infernal Proserpine; the Eleusians their ancient goddess Ceres; some Juno, other Bellona, other Hecate, other Rhamnusia, and principally both sort of Ethiopians which dwell in the Orient and are enlightened by the morning rays of the sun, and the Egyptians, which are excellent in all kind of ancient doctrine, and by their proper ceremonies accustom to worship me, do call me by my true name, Queen Isis.'

Isis instructs Lucius to attend a public ceremony of hers the following day, when the High Priest will be carrying a wreath of roses for him as a result of being instructed to do so in a vision that she will give him.

This occurs, and Lucius resumes his human form, becomes a three-fold initiate in the Mysteries of Isis and Osiris, of which he says he can tell us nothing save that:

I approached the very gates of death and set one foot on Proserpine's threshold, yet was permitted to return, rapt through all the elements. At midnight I saw the sun shining as if it were noon; I entered the presence of the gods of the underworld and the gods of the upper world, stood near and worshipped them.

The solemn rites end at dawn and he emerges from the sanctuary wearing twelve different stoles—no doubt corresponding to the wholeness of the zodiacal signs, elsewhere symbolized by the initiatory twelve labours of Hercules, the archetypal man.

However, we have in fact been told much by Apuleius in the guise of the asses' adventures, which in the guise of a low vulgar story have preserved high initiatory secrets for nigh on two millennia.

Part Five:
The Tibetan Experience:
An Eastern Perspective

We have examined the dynamics of the Mysteries of the Rose Cross and the Goddess from three Western perspectives; that of ancient pre-Olympian Greek mythology; that of seventeenth-century Rosicrucian alchemy; and that of the Mysteries of Isis at the beginnings of the Christian epoch. We propose now to look at an oriental system as expounded in the Mahayana Buddhism of Tibet.

The pre-Olympian Greek encapsulates the pre-historic Western traditions; the Apuleian Mysteries of Isis encapsulate the best of the classical pagan heritage; and the alchemical Rosicrucian the esoteric wisdom of Western Christian civilization. The contribution of Tibet is a valuable and unique one, deriving from the physical isolation of that country, which preserved a virtually medieval theocratic society into modern times.

A key figure in making the Tibetan wisdom accessible and realizing its significance was the American-Welsh scholar W. Y. Evans-Wentz. All of his writings are well worth study. His first major book was published in 1911, entitled *The Fairy Faith in Celtic Countries*. Its dual dedication is not without significance. First to A.E. (George Russell) 'whose unwavering loyalty to the fairy-faith has inspired much that I have herein written, whose friendly guidance in my study of the Irish mysticism I most gratefully acknowledge'. And also to W. B. Yeats, 'who brought to me at my own alma mater in California the first message from Fairyland and who afterwards in his own country led me through the haunts of fairy kings and queens.' Although the book was developed from an academic paper presented to the University of Rennes and then to the University of Oxford, Evans-Wentz's dedicatory sentiments are obviously those of one who had penetrated the Mysteries at first hand, and who has ventured well beyond the confines of the library and the scholarly intellect.

His book is a collection of beliefs and traditions of the fairy world, collected from Ireland, Scotland, Wales, Brittany, Cornwall and the Isle of Man. He presents them with the idea that they contain elements of a pre-Christian religion. Kathleen Raine notes in her foreword to a recent paperback edition:

> . . . in what W.B. Yeats calls 'the desolate places', furthest removed from the influences of modern civilisation, the oral tradition of unlettered country people has preserved elements of the religion of a learned caste, the Druids, whom Pythagoras himself honoured as custodians of esoteric knowledge. Elements of earlier and later faiths and local circumstances have coloured this immemorial doctrine of the unseen world only superficially: in essence the author believes that the old religion is grounded in the unchanging nature of things visible and invisible common to all traditions. In all times and places, with the sole exception of our own machine-made world, the universe is held to be living. The visible is but the outer aspect of the one life, diversified into spiritual beings, energies and agencies of many kinds. Of this world-wide animism the fairy-faith is an expression. It is a doctrine of souls; of the inter-relation of those two worlds, each 'dying the other's life, living the other's death' of which Plato and Plotinus taught.

Evans-Wentz did not pursue his researches into Celtic Studies. He found a natural extension to them, in a complete and intellectually satisfying form, in the mystical traditions of Tibet. Thereafter he produced a series of translations of texts that pioneered the latter day interest in Tibetan Mahayana Buddhism.

These works are *The Tibetan Book of the Dead; Tibet's Great Yogi Milrepa; Tibetan Yoga and Secret Doctrines* and *The Tibetan Book of the Great Liberation.* All these books have retained their importance despite the publication of more modern texts such as Lama Govinda's *Foundations of Tibetan Mysticism,* Detleg Ingo

Lawf's *Secret Doctrine of the Tibetan Books of the Dead*, and works by the Dalai Lama and other Tibetans expelled by the Chinese invasion of 1959.

The serious student is recommended to study these works but we shall here endeavour to summarize the gist of Tibetan Mahayana Buddhism as it relates to the Mystery Traditions we have been discussing. The similarities between the Tibetan system and that of the Celts is quite remarkable. Indeed it has led some esoteric savants, including the greatly respected Ronald Hever, to postulate an inner link between the British Isles and Tibet. Be this as it may, there is a strong similarity between the circled cross and its central focus, and the structure of the soul and inner worlds as expounded in *The Tibetan Book of the Dead.*

The purpose of *The Tibetan Book of the Dead* is for recitation to one who is dying. This is performed by a priest trained and dedicated to the function. He continues to recite it after actual physical death. This is because it is the soul that is being addressed, which is still in the vicinity of the corpse. According to Tibetan belief, the newly dead still hears much of what is being said on the physical level, the function of hearing persisting for some period after physical death.

The purpose of the ritual is to direct the attention of the soul to key images that will open a pathway for it away from the recurrent cycle of rebirth and death. It is held that immediately at the moment of death there is a unique opportunity to escape this wheel by focusing attention to its centre.

If the opportunity is lost, then another stage follows when attention to the spiritual images about a symbolic wheel, in the four cardinal directions, will still be highly efficacious.

In these two stages we have a replica of the magic circle and equal armed cross that we have considered at the beginning of this book.

The images are, however, in oriental form. That is, of a buddha—or ideal man—visualized in a different colour at each station, and with different symbolic attributes. Each buddha also has a feminine counterpart or companion, often in intimate embrace, thus giving a polar completeness to the whole imagery.

The central realm of the Tibetan magic circle is known as the Spreading Forth of the Seed, and the buddha seen here is of radiant white light, seated on a throne supported by lions and bearing a golden wheel of eight spokes. This eight-fold wheel denotes manifest life and the noble eight-fold way of properly conducting oneself. It also signifies the eight *siddhis* or occult worldly attainments. These are invincibility against all evil; vision of all the worlds; swiftness in going to or through them; ability to take on any form within them; eternal youth; ability to reduce oneself to a spiritual point; ability to pass through all barriers of form; power over treasures and spirits of the lower worlds. Combined, these form the highest attainment of all, that of universal sovereignty, and recognition as an exemplar and teacher.

The name of this central buddha is Bhagavan Vairechana. He represents the father and seed of all that is and he is embraced by the Divine Mother of Infinite Space, also called the Sovereign Lady of Heavenly Space (according to translation). She is known as Akasa Dhath Ishvari, and represents the feminine principle in the Universe. From the heart of this buddha and his consort there radiates the blue light of heavenly wisdom.

We pass now to the four buddhas of the cardinal directions and their associated female counterparts or *dakinis*.

In the East, the Realm of Pre-eminent Happiness, is Bhagavan Vajra-Sattva Akshobhya, who is pictured as blue in colour, seated on a throne supported by elephants, and holding a five pronged dorje. The dorje is a Tibetan form of magic wand, being a thunderbolt sceptre. For Westerners this could equally be regarded as a wand, with a star or pentagram at its tip; a five-pointed star that has all the implications and power of the Lightning Flash of the Qabalistic Tree of Life that traces the descent of force from the heights of creative power. This buddha is known as the hero-minded one, or one of indestructible mind. In short, he is a veritable Heracles. He is embraced by Mamiki the Divine Mother, and from them radiates the white light of the principle of consciousness.

In the South, the Glorious Realm, we find Bhagavan Ratna-Sambhava, a buddha visualized in yellow. He is called the beautiful one born of a jewel, and in fact bears a precious gem, and is seated on a throne supported by horses. He is embraced by another form of the Divine Mother, known as Sangyay-Chauma, she of the buddha (or enlightened) eyes. From them there radiates a dazzling yellow radiance of the wisdom of equality.

In the West, the Realm of Happiness, is pictured in red Bhagavan Buddha Amitabha, bearing a lotus blossom, and seated on a peacock throne. He is known as the one of the Boundless and Incomprehensible Light, or of Life Eternal, and is embraced by the Divine Mother Gokarmo—the white robed one. From them emanates the red light of discriminating wisdom.

In the North, which is the Realm of the Successful Performance of the Possible Actions, is visualized in green Bhagavan Buddha Amogha-Siddhi—the Almighty Conqueror—bearing crossed dorjes. This is the Tibetan image of supreme achievement and power, being in itself a form of the circled cross. He sits on a throne supported by harpies—or winged goddesses. His consort is the Divine Mother Talma, known as the feminine Saviour. From them emanates the green radiance of Wisdom in action.

We therefore find that we have an Eastern replica of our Western magic circle symbolism. It is useful to ponder upon the related symbolism and to realize that different cultures will produce different forms of it, in terms of symbolic instruments and colours, based upon the same geometric form. The student should overcome the natural but pointless anxiety over minor variations of symbolic attribution. This causes needless difficulty for the beginner and even friction between adherents of particular schools and systems. The experienced practitioner knows that any of the principal variations can be used following upon a decision of the spiritual will to use any particular one. It is only lack of expression of the spiritual will that causes the vacillation and indecision of the neophyte, that is sometimes alternatively expressed by a travesty of the spiritual will in emotive dogmatic assertion.

The Tibetan system proceeds to elaborate very considerably upon the five-fold wheel. In *The Tibetan Book of the Dead*, there follows a succession of 'peaceful' and 'wrathful' deities, but the system is too complex for us to examine in detail.

Briefly, the schema is that the newly deceased has a unique opportunity at the time of actual physical death. For this moment by its very nature coincides with the proximity and appearance of the in-most spiritual principle that is manifested in the radiant white and blue central buddha and dakini. Identity with this emerging effulgence will take one straight to the uncreate heaven worlds, with no further entanglement in the form worlds or the cycle of birth and death.

If one fails to seize this opportunity then the next best thing is to identify with the four-fold circle of the buddhas and dakinis of the four cardinal directions. These correspond to the arms of the equal armed cross of the Western system that we have outlined. This period, which is said to last three or four days, is the time when the 'awareness body' is being formulated for perception and experience on the astral plane. In other words when this body is being created there is an opportunity to make direct contact with the pure high forces of creation beyond the form worlds.

Following this stage, and corresponding to about a week of earthly time, there are visions of the assembly of a formation of forty-two peaceful deities; and then of fifty-eight wrathful deities. It is emphasized that all these are emanations or creations of oneself, and not exterior entities. The purpose of a life of meditation on earth is in fact to prepare oneself for dealing with these projections. Thus the *Book of the Dead* is a manual of initiation for the living as well as a guide book for the deceased.

There follows a period of about a month (although these time intervals are symbolic rather than literal) concerned with the soul going forth through the *bardo* (or astral plane) in an experiential journey prior to being drawn back to physical rebirth at an appropriate place and time.

All this is in direct parallel to the Western system that we have outlined. In life, the circled cross, or the rose cross, may be meditated upon as a healing, integrating symbol. Its central core, the rose of direct mystical experience is, in essence, more valid and partaking of 'ultimate' reality than even the four-fold balancing of the elemental principles redeemed in equilibrium.

Beyond this core structure are the manifold experiences and expressions of human consciousness, which range from the diverse expressions of virtue (as in Dante's *Paradiso*) to the diverse expressions of vice (as in Dante's *Inferno*) though there is a way in between symbolically expressed in Dante's *Purgatorio*.

The detail of Dante's great fourteenth-century work can be hard going for the modern student but it is, properly understood, a Western equivalent of *The Tibetan Book of the Dead*. Central to, and at the core, of Dante's great symbolic vision is the *rosa mystica*; a great white rose floating in its own fragrance in the Empyreum, with God at its centre and the essence of creation in all its purity as the petals. Essentially, uncreate reality is formless. This central fact is not forgotten in the Tibetan cosmogony, as we shall see.

The Tibetan system is a complex interlocking one, and the various experiences of *The Tibetan Book of the Dead* have their correlation with various psychic centres in the subtle body.

Thus the central buddha of ultimate reality, the Compassionate One, corresponds to the centre above the head; the 'peaceful deities' relate to the heart; the 'wrathful deities' to the head; the wisdom bearers of the balanced cross relate to the throat; and the dagger bearing guardian of these Mysteries to the centre of the generative organs and perineum. The dakinis of the buddhas are associated with the solar plexus; whilst the underworld powers are at the soles of the feet.

There is also a related analysis of the types of being to be found in the form worlds. Besides humans, there are 'gods', 'titans', animals, ghosts and the denizens of hell. In fact we might tabulate these correspondences, alongside the great mantrum of Eastern mysticism.

		above the head	boddhisattva (saviour, Compassionate One)
OM	gods	forehead	wrathful deities (intellectual analysis, contention)
MA	titans	throat	wisdom gods
NE	humans	heart	peaceful deities (love)
PAD	animals	solar plexus	wisdom goddesses
ME	hungry ghosts	genitals	dagger bearing guardian
HUM	hell	feet	denizens of hell

Sometimes these categories are depicted in circular form, the topmost at the centre of a six-rayed wheel containing the other categories. The whole wheel is seen to move in the grasp of a ferocious looking deity who commands all the illusory form worlds, and who is known as Mara.

However, a more comprehensive schema, that includes the 'higher' formless worlds as well as the worlds of form, is the Mount Meru system. This, like the Tree of Life of the West, through the aid of pictorial imagery assists the mind to comprehend something of the whole, and the inter-relationship of parts in the inner worlds.

The image of Mount Meru is a complex glyph that comprehends within its symbolism all the worlds, from the deepest hells of hatred and delusion to the greatest formless heights of abounding grace and love. It is thus, par excellence, a model or three-dimensional solid map of the universe, inner and outer, formless and formed. It is depicted as a great four-sided mountain, ascending into the heights of space, with the city of the gods at the summit, and the ordinary worlds of men at its base.

It stands at the top of a great iron mountain in the centre of a seven-fold crater of clear sweet lakes and circular mountain ranges. Beyond these is a circular salt sea in which are four island continents, at each of the cardinal directions around the central island of Mount Meru. These four continents, a mere one of which represents the whole physical universe as we know it, represent different modes of human existence. The particular continent representing the current human condition is to the South of Mount Meru and is known as Jambu Island.

Deep within the iron landmass are the various hells of the evil doers. Whilst they are perhaps not as comprehensive in their imagery as Dante's vision of hell, their various degrees of hotness and coldness and forms of torment, fit the particular form of vice to which they are appropriate. We should state that all hellish punishment, in Western or Eastern esoteric systems, is self-inflicted and a result of a continued voluntary embracing of evil. It is not, as in popular ideas of medieval theology, a rigorous punishment from a vindictive and merciless deity. The fact is that those who give themselves to hatred, greed, lust or any of the moral vices, will, in time or out of time, find themselves surrounded by an objective state that corresponds to their interior condition. Strange as it may seem, we get what we desire. The court of Yama, the Lord of the Dead, reigns supreme in a hall of justice over the system of hells. These are often classified into sixteen different hells (eight hot and eight cold) each with sixteen appendices. The deepest hell is as far down in the iron mountain as the peak of Mount Meru rises above it.

Various entities share the worlds of men. They include the angelic and elemental oversouls or guardians of various parts of the earth's surface: rivers, springs, woods, trees, hills and so forth. These are conceived in the generic title of *nagas*, or *asuras*, or divine animals. They have at their highest level much in common with Western god forms and archetypes. At the lowest level they are conceived as 'hungry ghosts', wandering the earth, or just under its surface, tormented by unsatiated greeds or desires. On reflection it will be realized that most ghosts are indeed hungry for something, and the adjective invariably accompanies the noun in Tibetan mysticism.

Mount Meru, rising four square out of the centre of the seven-fold ring system of mountain peaks and cool clear lakes, is the abode of higher forms of consciousness. The four sides of the holy mountain are each of a specific jewel—emerald, crystal, lapis lazuli and ruby. It stands between the Sun and Moon and its peak rises into the clouds and formless realms above the sun and moon.

The lower slopes of the holy mountain are known as the heaven of the Four Great Kings. These are divine beings of a relatively minor order who regulate the form worlds. In the West they would correspond to orders of angels and archangels.

At the top of the holy mountain is the City of the Gods, and within it Indra's Palace—a place of surpassing beauty and delight and which might be compared, in the West, with the New Jerusalem, or the uncorrupted Garden of Eden, the Earthly Paradise.

There are various levels of heavenly existence, however, just as there are in Dante's *Paradiso*, and all of them represent various modes of perfect expression in the worlds of form. However, beyond the topmost towers of the palace of the chief of all the gods, there extend, into and beyond the skies, the formless worlds. These are variously known as the Buddha Fields, the Mythic Lands, or the Pure Lands of the Buddhas. Their equivalent in Western systems of exegesis would be the

Ain Soph beyond Kether on the Tree of Life; or the Divine Empyreum in which there floats the Mystic Rose in Dante's *Divine Comedy*.

There are various ways by which man can aspire to these higher realms, and these are represented by various spiritual disciplines and ways of meditation, ranging from the form discipline of yoga to the formless disciplines of mystical contemplation.

In the Tibetan System the way of Mahayana Buddhism is conceived as the greatest. Others are Hinayana Buddhism, the disciplines of Hindu esotericism, and the ancient nature-based esoteric system known as Bön. In Western terms these correspond to devotional mysticism (Hinayana), where personal salvation is sought; esoteric meditation and yoga (Hinduism) wherein higher self-knowledge and control is sought; and the nature mysticism of the Craft (Bön) which seeks communion with Nature as the luminous garment of the creator.

Mahayana represents a higher form of Path in that it seeks to redeem or raise the rest of nature by its efforts. It is thus a way of 'Christification', even though the term Christ is not used. In this system the one who achieves buddhahood does not go on to the formless worlds, but waits at the threshold of form with the intention of helping on those who have yet to achieve. It is thus a Path which has compassion and vicarious redemption at the apex of its aspiration. In this it is identical with the highest aims of Western esotericism.

The buddha soul may even return to the worlds of form, not driven to or drawn therein by bonds of karma, but voluntarily taking on the karma of others. In this form he would be known as a boddhisattva. In this respect the Incarnation of Christ may be looked upon as a supreme example of this general principle. And the texts of Tibetan buddhism may be regarded as treatises on white magic. The principles and methodology are the same. They differ only in the detail of their symbolism.

Part Six:
The Return of the Goddess

Tibetan perceptions are particularly interesting in their recognition of the feminine principle, and the fact that the forces of death and of sex are similar.

In astrology the sign Scorpio (or the Eighth House) is held to rule over both sexual expression and death. Primitive mystery and religious systems also derive from blood sacrifice and orgy as their two poles. To penetrate the mysteries of the forces that lie beyond physical life there are the two avenues that we discussed at the beginning of this book. One is the attempt to go on beyond death into the earth or the tomb. The other is to attempt to get back to conditions before birth via woman or the womb.

In terms of the symbolism of the circled cross, this may be expressed by placing gateways at North and South. To be within physical incarnation is to be in the Western half of the circle. Then the two gateways form two alternative ways of penetrating the Eastern, inner half. The Northern gateway leads through the tomb, the Southern gateway back through the womb.

As we have said, the primitive techniques for this were blood sacrifice and orgiastic rites but neither of these methods are valid means of spiritual progress nowadays. The evolution of consciousness has moved on and such practices would be atavistic; degrading rather than enlightening.

There is a third way, and that is the approach to the centre—the centre of the spiral. That is, to the mid-point of the web of creation. Here may be found a very ancient feminine symbol in the spider who spins and designs and builds the web of manifestation. The symbol is also found in Rosicrucian diagrams.

She represents in other symbolic formulations the Three Sisters, the Fates, spinning, weaving and cutting the thread of life. Whoever becomes a victim of the spider is, when bound and eaten by her, transformed. She is also the sleeping Lady Venus who, if awakened, gives birth to a King. Whoever has found her secret door is translated from questing querent into guardian of her Mysteries. In other words a change of function, or a transformation, takes place.

This is expressed in Arthurian legend in various stories of knights who come to the place of a fountain, very often in a grove of trees. Here, in a forbidding ambience of threatening danger (knights' bones, rusting armour, decapitated heads) the questing knight makes his presence and challenging intention known by blowing a horn, or striking a shield, or pouring water from a cup to a rock, which may bring thunderous roarings and lightnings.

In another form it is the challenge to the dragon, which in popular story sees the knight as fighting in order to rescue an enchained maiden. In other versions it may be a serpent/dragon who lives at the base of a tree who has to be confronted. Or the feminine form may come forth as the Faery Queen, willing to guide the questor through the inner worlds to the magic mountain—often significantly called the Venusburg or Mountain of Venus.

Other examples of variations can be culled from the varieties of symbolism, apart from those we have examined in our discussion of ancient Greek mythology, *The Chymical Marriage of Christian Rosencreutz*, or *The Golden Ass* of Apuleius. Indeed the principle is a universal one; it is found in a multitude of sources, from fairy tale and folk song to the Book of Genesis.

In Genesis it has been given a curiously anti-feminine bias. The Hebrew scribes and prophets distorted their primitive tradition in an attempt to square it with their later perceived destiny. Similarly Paul of Tarsus, as a deeply committed Pharisaic Jew, could not quite shake off his personal conditioning when giving spiritual direction to the early Christian Church. He undervalued the role of the feminine in any function apart from the dutiful and passive, and Western culture has suffered considerably from these distortions.

However, the karmic roots go deeper than this, to very deep seated factors long before Paul. It should not be forgotten that the pagan Mysteries were also paternalistic and masculine orientated, despite the worship of the goddess. Initiates were not only male, but from the higher echelons of society. It was an exclusive élitism far removed from modern democratic and egalitarian assumptions. Indeed it was a scandal to the pagan world that Christianity opened up its Mysteries to women and to slaves. However, it is instructive to look closely at the Christian story to see the function of women within it. Who stood at the foot of the cross? Who was first at the tomb on the morning of the Resurrection?

The dark figure of the mother at the foot of the sacrificial cross is more than a mourning Jewish woman. She is this too, for in the Christian story the universal finds expression in the particular. Yet she is also a representative of the great dark Mother of Form, who gave birth to the Saviour, and now stands under the wood of the cross to witness his passage through the gates of death. Jesus had presented his challenge and his credentials on the olive-clad mount of the Garden of Gethsemene. He has crossed the brook Kedron between worlds of existence, and their values. He has met the dragon in the form of the mob, with its dual heads of priestly and secular power. Now he enters the Underworld, between the pillars of two other crosses, for a three-day journey from Good Friday to Easter Sunday.

The Passion of Jesus Christ is indeed a Mystery story, a process of Initiation. But it is more than this. It is unique as a once for all cosmic event, taking place at a point in time and space, in the body of the Earth. It raised the spiritual quality and opportunity of planetary life.

At the same time it is a pattern for others to follow. In this it is a way of initiation, and one that is followed not only by convinced Christians. It appears under other names in other cultures and traditions, such as the buddhas and boddhisattvas of the Mahayana traditions of Tibet, amongst others. Indeed these other traditions, in that they may be free of particular Western cultural limitations or intellectual assumptions, may have much to teach. There is a hidden Christ in Buddhism, in Hinduism, in the pagan religions, as St Augustine himself observed.

The feminine principle has gradually broken through the hard crust of masculine bias throughout the Christian centuries. The gospels themselves make very little of the mother of Jesus. She is referred to but twice in the earliest gospel, that of Mark.

The earliest Biblical reference to Mary is in Paul's letter to the Galatians (Chapter 4), when he refers to Jesus as being 'born of a woman'. There is however more to this remark than a passing reference to the mother of Jesus. Paul is talking of the previous immaturity of man, whom he describes as being no more than a child in cosmic terms. 'During our minority we were slaves to the elemental spirits of the universe.' But this phase is now over for 'God has sent his own son, born of a woman, born under the law, to purchase the freedom of the subjects of the law, in order that we might attain the status of sons'. In other words the possibility now arrives of achieving freedom from the cyclic law of birth and death. Following upon the talismanic action of the Incarnation of the Christ, the bearer of infinite Cosmic Love, new levels of reality are now available to human beings.

'To prove that you are sons, God has sent into your hearts the Spirit of his Son, crying "Abba! Father!" You are therefore no longer a slave but a son, and if a son, then also by God's own act an heir.'

He goes on to be more specific, for the Galatians—an ethnic group deriving originally from Celtic Gaul—were reluctant to abandon their old gods. 'Formerly,' he says, 'when you did not acknowledge God, you were the slaves of beings which in their nature are no gods. But now that you do acknowledge God—or rather, now that he has acknowledged you—how can you turn back to the mean and beggarly spirits of the elements? Why do you propose to enter their service all over again? You keep special days and months and seasons and years. You make me fear all the pains I spent on you may prove to be labour lost.'

Considerable misunderstanding has been caused by the need for Paul, the apostle to the Gentiles, to preach *against* the old gods that currently held sway. Their priests and adherents were blind to, and naturally suspicious of, the new spiritual insights. However, the Christ came to fulfil, not to overthrow. And the correct way through would have been a Christ-orientated consolidation and unification of the old religions.

This was realized by great Neo-Platonic teachers of the early Christian era such as Plotinus (who is far too little studied) and the writers of the Hermetic scripts. They sought a way forward by grafting the new revelation onto the old pagan aspirations. There was really no reason to try to limit the new revelation to a form of neo-Judaism.

This problem soon split the early Church. One party wished to exclude all non-Jews from the faith. Or if they were to be admitted, that it should be only on condition that they accept the whole of the Jewish religious law and ritual observances, including circumcision. However it was still a long time before the Church could come to terms with the symbols and powers of the feminine principle.

This principle, or the Goddess, is at root the feminine side of the Deity. It is something much more than any individual pagan goddess, though the Egyptian goddess Isis, with her ability to absorb many other goddesses of the ancient world, came close to representing the total principle.

In Qabalistic terms the roots of the Feminine are in the very grounds of form. In the manifest universe these are embodied in the symbolism of the Sephirah Binah and in the unmanifest reality beyond, in the Great Sea (Marah) of the Ain Soph (the Limitless).

The first chapter of Genesis describes the same thing in the image of great waters of an as yet unmanifest Earth: 'And the Earth was without form and void: and darkness was upon the face of the deep. And the Spirit of God moved upon the face of the waters.'

Other forms of this concept are to be found in ancient references to the Cosmic Egg. We could also cite the 'Stanzas of Dzyan', to which H. P. Blavatsky went for inspiration, and which form the core of *The Secret Doctrine*. From Stanza I: 'The Eternal Parent wrapped in her ever-invisible robes had slumbered once again for seven Eternities.' Let us take note of the feminine gender ascribed to the Eternal parent.

And from Stanza III: 'The last vibration of the seventh Eternity thrills through Infinitude. The Mother swells, expanding from within without, like the bud of the lotus. The vibration sweeps along touching with its swift wing the whole universe, and the Germ that dwelleth in Darkness; the Darkness that breathes over the slumbering Waters of Life. "Darkness" radiates Light, and Light drops one solitary Ray into the Mother-deep. The Ray shoots through the virgin Egg, the Ray causes the eternal Egg to thrill and drop the non-Eternal Germ, which condenses into the World-egg.'

Other ancient cosmogonies can be cited for an appreciation of this primordial feminine principle. For instance, the ancient Greek shepherd poet Hesiod, of the eighth century B.C.

'In the beginning,' he wrote, 'there was Chaos vast and dark.' The term Chaos comes from a root meaning 'to gape' and thus designates open space. Later, confusion arose because of a false derivation from a word meaning 'to pour', so that the word came to mean a confused and disorganized mess. The meaning of Hesiod for Chaos is a cosmic principle of pure eternal space. This, however, is the Cosmic Mother of All.

Kerenyi translates from Hesiod's *Theogony* as follows: 'Then arose broad-breasted Gaia, the firm and everlasting abode of all divinities, those that dwell high above, on Mount Olympus, and those that dwell within her, in the earth, likewise Eros, the loveliest of the immortal gods, who loosens the limbs and rules the spirit of all gods and men. From chaos are descended Erebos, the lightless darkness of the depths; and Nyx, Night. Nyx in love with Erebos, bore Aither, the light of heaven, and Hemera, the day. Gaia, for her part, bore, first of all and as her equal, the starry Sky, Ouranos, so that he should completely cover her and be a firm and everlasting abode for the blessed gods. She bore the great Mountains, whose valleys are favourite dwellings of goddesses—the Nymphs. She bore also that desolate foaming Sea, the Pontos. And all those she bore without Eros, without mating.'

To Ouranos she later bore the Titans and other creatures that we have already discussed earlier in this book and which have their oriental correspondences in the various gods, asuras, and divine animals of the Buddhist Mount Meru system.

All of the great principles of femininity here embodied are notably and painfully lacking from the Hebraic Old Testament, except perhaps in the Wisdom literature of Solomon.

In *A Practical Guide to Qabalistic Symbolism* we defined the Sephirah Binah as follows: 'Binah is the form giver to all manifestation and thus also is the Archetypal Temple behind all temples, the Inner Church behind all churches, the Basic Creed behind all creeds. It is the Womb of Life, and this archetypal feminine quality of the Sephirah manifests in two aspects, as Ama, the dark sterile mother, and Aima, the bright fertile mother.'

In the Christian mythos the Blessed Virgin, Mary the Mother of God, becomes the vehicle for both these aspects. In the bright vernal scene of the Annunciation, when the Archangel Gabriel comes to her, bearing lilies, and seeks her gracious permission to be the bearer of the infant god-head, and she says yes—'Be it unto me according to thy Word'—grace and jest combined, she is the archetypal embodiment of the Bright Fertile Mother. In a sense this is a transformation and fulfilment of the great pagan virgin goddesses such as Diana or Atalanta.

In terms of Hebraic letter symbolism Ama is composed of the Hebrew letter Mem, which signifies water, the Waters of Form, between two Alephs, signifying the beginnings of things (or the driving power therein). Aima is the same word with the fertilizing Yod impacted within it.

The Dark Sterile Mother is embodied in the image of Mary as mourning Mother, draped in black, standing at the foot of the cross upon which her son and God is impaled in death agony.

We have described elsewhere the great image of the Mother of Sorrows (*Practical Guide to Qabalistic Symbolism*, Vol. 1, Ch. VIII, pp. 21–24) in what were in fact quotations from an inner plane source. 'She can be seen as a mighty maternal figure of majesty and sorrow, robed in black, and seated in the centre of a sphere of purple light, graduating from translucent violet and lilac to the deep purple of grapes in the centre—an excellent symbol in itself for it signifies one who has trod the winepress alone. The figure can be considered as Christian or pagan, for the sorrow of the feminine side of the Divinity is the same through the ages, whether it be Demeter sorrowing for her daughter, Ishtar descending the seven hells for her lover, Isis searching for the dismembered parts of her husband, or Mary watching her son die.

'On the higher levels the Sorrow of Binah is the knowledge and understanding of the great cosmic factors behind the incarnation of man and also of Christ. It is the realization and revelation of the Great Mother herself. An awareness of this condition can be made by building the picture of the Crucifixion with Our Lady and St John on either side of the Cross. The skies are seen to grow black and the Crucifixion takes place between earth and sky in some strange condition of space. Mary herself steps forward as if to take on herself the weight of the symbolism, and overshadowing all is Tzaphkiel, the Archangel of Binah, and the deep crimson, black, dark brown and grey flecked pink of the Sephirah's colours.

'This image should lead to an understanding of the whole of the manifested Universe as a form encompassing pure cosmic force; a gigantic Cross upon which this force is crucified. And the whole of life is lived under the Shadow of this Cross. This is the primary Cross of Life of which the Cross of Golgotha is a lesser manifestation; a shadow cast by the Great Shadow.

'Contemplation of Binah may bring a very real sense of being surrounded by Great Waters, and in this connection the Temple of Binah is an Ark upon the Supernal Seas. This is the "Ark of Isis", a symbol of the Womb of the Great Mother.'

This symbol of the Ark of Isis or the Moon Ark is one of very great protection and is of immense antiquity, sometimes being associated with a Moon Tree. The earliest representation of the moon god (and by extension this means the Feminine Divine Principle) are to be found in cones or pillars of stone, often of meteoric origin, sometimes carved and sometimes left un-worked.

These are not phallic stones, although they are sometimes confused with them. When such a pillar is made of wood we have the Moon Tree, examples of which are found illustrated in Dr Esther Harding's *Woman's Mysteries*, an important text for anyone who wishes to understand the psychological implications of the goddess.

It is these great Feminine powers that gradually begin to make themselves felt and to assert their presence, despite the world view of Judaic Christianity, that at first almost completely excluded the female principle, and even saw it as the root of all evil in the figure of Eve. However, in the dramatis personae of the Garden of Eden story, there are all the elements for redemption through the feminine principle. The serpent and the tree in the Garden are familiar figures from the Garden of the Hesperides.

The gradual increase in the realization of the importance of the divine feminine principle can be traced over the twenty centuries of Christendom. It is one that develops in parallel with the evolution of human consciousness. Indeed humanity itself, in one sense, may be looked upon as the Bride. Indeed the Blessed Virgin Mary also represents each individual human soul, preparing itself for the 'cosmic marriage'. With this in mind, the increasing importance of the Cult of Mary becomes an important indicator of the evolution of human consciousness in the West.

From the unpromising beginnings in the Synoptic gospels, where even the nativity stories relating to Mary are thought to be later interpolations, we find, by the second century, the appearance of the apocryphal gospels of The Book of James and the Gospel of Thomas, which attempted to fulfil a natural demand for details of the 'Mother of God'.

This process has been condemned as a 'throw back' to paganism; a view which is as shallow as it is narrow. The process is rather an enrichment, an expansion of inner truth. A realization that the historical life and death of Jesus Christ was a talismanic act of astounding significance and vast proportions. It was the overshadowing of inner forces to a unique degree. The full truth of this can only be realized by a gradual expansion of human consciousness and even then only in symbolic terms. Hence the stories of Mary are not 'mere mythologizing' but a gradual filtering through of profound metaphysical truths about the cosmic place and function of the feminine principle. The image of the Blessed Virgin is the new Isis, if one may so phrase it. The raising of her status from simple Jewish virgin to Queen of Heaven has been a gradual process of realization of the cosmic destiny of the human race.

This was all foreshadowed in the Canticles of Solomon, the great lover king and builder of the original Temple. It is also found in the Revelation of John of Patmos, and his vision of the New Jerusalem, decked as a Bride.

It may help to summarize the gradual unfolding of this process of the emergence of the feminine principle.

By AD 200 paintings of the Virgin Mary were appearing in the catacombs of Rome which sheltered the early Christians, and the Book of James had been written. This dealt with the birth of

Mary herself, which in its own way was attended by prodigies, in that her Mother Anna is barren until she is visited by an angel in her garden. The tale is a poignant one. The visitation occurs while her husband Joachim is wandering in penance in the desert for forty days. His offerings to the Temple had been rejected by the High Priest who interpreted their continuing childlessness as a sign of the Lord's displeasure. In the absence of her husband the distressed Anna dresses herself in her old bridal array and wanders into the garden. She sits under a bay tree and becomes more distressed at the sight of a nestful of baby sparrows within its branches. Then the angel appears and promises her a child. At the same time an angel appears to Joachim who rushes back in joy, to be met by his wife at the golden gate of Jerusalem.

Their child, Mary, is dedicated to the Temple. She walks seven steps at the age of six months, and her mother catches her up, vowing that she shall walk no more upon the ground until she is taken to the Temple. Thereafter her bedchamber is made into a sanctuary, nothing common or unclean is taken into it, and the infant is tended and carried by dedicated maidens.

When she is one year old her father holds a great feast and she is blessed by the high priests at a great assembly of the priests, scribes, elders and people of Israel.

At her third year, in a ceremony involving a procession of virgins with lights, the child Mary is taken and dedicated to the Temple. Here she sits upon the third step of the altar, and then, filled with the grace of God, dances before the assembled people.

The priest who receives her makes a speech of welcome and dedication that is close to the Magnificat in wording and intention: 'The Lord hath magnified thy name among all generations; in thee in the latter days shall the Lord make manifest his redemption unto the children of Israel.'

Mary is hereafter described as being like a nurtured dove, fed by the hand of an angel.

When she reaches the age of twelve a council of priests is held to decide what is to be done with her, as it will not be possible for her to remain in the temple when she reaches puberty. The High Priest, in prayer in the Holy of Holies, is instructed by an angel to call together all the widowers of the people of Israel.

Each one is to bring his staff and a sign will follow showing which shall take Mary as his wife.

In due course all the widowers assemble, with their rods, including the carpenter Joseph. The rods are taken in and then returned, at which point a dove appears at the head of Joseph's staff and alights upon his head. He is therefore regarded as the chosen husband.

At first he strongly protests saying: 'I have sons, and I am an old man, but she is a girl: lest I become a laughing stock to the children of Israel.' However, the High Priest insists, warning Joseph against disobeying the Lord. Joseph therefore takes Mary into his house but does not lay with her as a husband.

Shortly afterwards there is a need for a veil to be made for the Temple, which is to be made by seven pure virgins of the Tribe of David. Mary is chosen to be one of these and, the tasks falling by lot, is appointed to spin and weave the purple and scarlet parts of the veil—the others being white, gold and hyacinthine colours.

In short, in this highly symbolic sequence, to her go the colours of kingship and blood in the Veil of the Temple, which is a thinly disguised form of the Veil of Isis, the veil of phenomenal appearance that cloaks inner reality.

Mary begins to spin the scarlet thread. She is thus a 'new age' representative of the age old Fates of pre-Olympian myth. Then she goes, in another re-enactment of ancient symbolism, to a source of water to fill her pitcher. Here the angel of the Annunciation appears to her, saying 'Hail, thou that art highly favoured; the Lord is with thee; blessed art thou among women.'

She returns to her house with the pitcher of water (a female Aquarian image if ever there was one) and there starts to spin the purple thread—the one signifying royalty—and the angel appears to her again. 'Fear not, Mary, for thou hast found grace before the Lord of all things, and thou shalt conceive of his word.'

Mary mentally questions this awesome statement. 'Shall I *really* conceive of the living God, and bring forth after the manner of all women?'

The angel then amplifies his statement, answering her unspoken thoughts. 'Not so, Mary, for a power of the Lord shall overshadow thee: wherefore also that holy thing which shall be born of thee shall be called the Son of the Highest. And thou shalt call his name Jesus: for he shall save his people from their sins.'

To which Mary replies, with the now time-honoured words. These epitomize the human soul, unsullied by sin, sounding forth a knowledge and acceptance of its destiny, in grace, faith and love. 'Behold the handmaid of the Lord is before him: be it unto me according to thy word.'

She then weaves the purple and scarlet thread and takes her portion of the veil to the priest—just as the purple and scarlet of the lineaments of the embryo of the god man are to be woven within her womb. The priest blesses her, saying: 'Mary, the Lord God hath magnified thy name, and thou shalt be blessed among all generations of the earth.'

Mary rejoices, and in due course visits her kinswoman Elizabeth who is to be mother of the fore-runner, John the Baptist. This story is taken up in the Gospel of Luke, but here the weaving symbolism is followed through, in that Mary finds Elizabeth weaving scarlet wool. (This is a symbolic comparison to the fine linen and silk with which she, as mother of the divine one, has worked.)

We have quoted at some length from the Gospel of James because it is representative of the first workings of 'tradition' in the growing Christian community, which at that time had little power and was subject to intermittent persecution at the hands of pagan authority.

From here on, as the Church grows, there is a gradual inexorable tide of the recognition of the importance of the Virgin and what she stands for. Before AD 400 we have the first recorded liturgies and invocation to her, and the legendary founding of the great shrines of St Maria Trastavere and St Maria Maggiore in Rome. By AD 500 the Temple of Isis at Soissons is dedicated to the Blessed Virgin Mary, as also the basilica at Salonika. The Feast of the Annunciation is kept at Byzantium (at the Vernal Equinox) and the Feast of the Commemoration of the Virgin is observed during Christmastide in Europe. In 431 the Council of Ephesus (the great old centre of Diana) proclaims her as *theotokos* (God bearer), and in 451 the Council of Chalcedon proclaims her as *aeiparthenos* (ever virgin). The Empress of Byzantium, in the middle of the fifth century, begins a collection of her relics.

By AD 600 the Parthenon at Athens—the temple of Pallas Athene, the goddess of wisdom, is dedicated to the Virgin Mary. A church of St Mary is founded in Jerusalem, the city of the original Temple of Solomon. And St Maria Antiqua is founded in Rome. In Byzantium, always a leader in recognition of the feminine principle, and where mosaics of the Virgin and Child had begun to replace those of Christ Pantocrator, the Feasts of the Nativity of the BVM, of her Presentation at the Temple, and the Dormitian or Falling Asleep of the BVM are being kept. The latter, which implies her freedom from the toils of death, falls on 15 August, one of the ancient Feast Days of Isis, when the Dog-Star Sirius rose to announce the eagerly awaited inundation of the Nile in Ancient Egypt that brought new life. Another ancient Isiac feast was commemorated on 15 February, the Festival of Lights, when little boats carrying lights were floated upon the waters. This became in the fourth century replaced by a Christian feast closely associated with Mary, the Presentation of Jesus in the Temple. This was the occasion of the moving testimony of the ancient Simeon: 'Lord, lettest thy servant depart in peace according to thy word, for mine eyes have seen thy salvation, which thou hast prepared before the face of all people; a light to lighten the Gentiles and the glory of thy people Israel.' When this Feast was recognized by Rome the emphasis became centred upon the purification of Mary herself. Through a change in calendarization the Feast of the Purification is now celebrated on 2 February.

The image of the Virgin also began to be used as a protection in battle. In 610 the Emperor Heraclius flew her banner at the masts of his battleships; in 626 the virgin and child were painted on the gates of the besieged Constantinople; and in 717 the same picture was paraded round the city walls to help repel the Arabs.

Pope Sergius I (687-701) instituted great candlelit processions in Rome on the major Marian Feast Days and John VII (705-7) took upon himself the title of 'servant of the Mother of God'. The Theophilus legend also began to circulate widely in the mid-eighth century, extolling the powers and virtues of the Virgin as protector against the works of the devil. The tale of Theophilus is of a sixth-century Faust figure, who allegedly made a pact, and sold his soul to the devil, via the offices of a Jewish necromancer, in return for worldly riches and success, after he had been passed over in ecclesiastical preferment. He was however saved by the Virgin.

By AD 900 a further dimension to the feminine principle was enacted in the institution of Feasts dedicated to the Mother of the Mother of God, St Anne. Although the cult of St Anne did not gain great force until the fifteenth and early sixteenth centuries, its seed appeared in the Institution of the Feast of the Conception of St Anne at Byzantium some six hundred years previously. At this time too, tradition has it that the Holy Roman Emperor, Charles the Bald, the son of Charlemagne, left in his will the treasured relic of the shift that Mary had worn at the Annunciation. It was to provide a fitting edifice for such a priceless gift that the present beautiful building of the cathedral of Notre Dame at Chartres was constructed in 1194, after the original church had been destroyed by fire, when the relic miraculously survived the conflagration.

It is easy for the modern secular mind to be cynical over such medieval beliefs but here is symbolic magic at work of the highest order. Qabalists will see the connections of the robe, the body's veil, with the principle of Binah, the archetypal feminine principle. And the fact that belief in this talismanic object should result in the building of a religious house of worship (in itself another Binah symbol) that is the jewel of Western Christendom, indicates a powerful reality at work on inner levels of expression.

By AD 1000, Saturdays were dedicated to the Blessed Virgin and one of her greatest shrines founded, the abbey of Montserrat in Catalonia. Here the focus of worship is a black madonna—and there are other shrines of considerable importance that have similar dark images, including Chartres, and St Maria Maggiore in Rome. Black Madonnas are particularly renowned for their wonder-working properties and have an ancient lineage in the Black Isis, who, in mourning for the lost Osiris in ancient Egyptian legend, was either black robed or herself black. In this guise, she was regarded as a goddess of healing, and the Black Madonnas have a similar reputation. In this aspect Isis is also patron of lovers because of her devoted seeking for Osiris, and the Black Madonna of Montserrat is particularly venerated by the newly married, for she is held to preside over sexual love, pregnancy and childbirth.

Other ancient dynamics of the feminine are associated with the Black Madonna of Montserrat. The image was allegedly found in a cave. Tradition has it that it was fashioned by St Luke, and given to St Peter, who took it to Spain. It had been hidden when the Moors invaded, and was subsequently revealed to a group of shepherds by a choir of angels. So much for tradition. In material terms the statue appears to be twelfth century Byzantine, though of unknown provenance. An interesting aspect of it is that, besides the infant Jesus, the Madonna has in her lap a Dionysian pine cone.

She carries sufficient power to have attracted immense wealth from the rulers of Barcelona, Aragon and Castile; and she also inspired St Ignatius of Loyola, the founder of the Jesuit Order, to abandon his military career in 1522, and become a soldier of Christ.

In the eleventh century there is evidence of the use of a form of rosary, although a precise date for the advent of this form of prayer is not known. It is generally assumed that the crusaders brought it back with them. In 1041 however, Lady Godiva of Coventry left a circlet of gems on which she used to say her prayers; and in the terms of her will she instructed that it be hung round a statue of the virgin. The rosary subsequently became a form of prayer pre-eminently associated with the Virgin.

The twelfth century was remarkable for the building of great cathedrals. A number of these were dedicated to St Mary, or Notre Dame. Famous ones are at Paris, Noyon, Laon, and a little later at Mantes, Coutances and Amiens. The temple, or holy place of worship, is as Qabalists will know, a symbol of the feminine principle. Of particular interest in this respect is the Holy House of Walsingham. This was built in 1130 following a vision in which the Virgin appeared to a Norman widow, Richeldis de Faverches. She was taken in the spirit to the house wherein Mary had received the Annunciation from the Archangel Gabriel, and raised the child Jesus. The measurements of the house were given to her, together with the instruction to build 'England's Nazareth'. This became a miraculous shrine until despoiled by Henry VIII four hundred years later.

Another important visionary of this time was Elisabeth of Schonan, a German nun, who, amongst other visions, saw the Virgin rising bodily to heaven. These visions achieved wide circulation and profoundly influenced ideas of the Assumption of the BVM which in time replaced earlier conceptions of the more passive Dormitian or falling asleep.

1251 saw another vision of the BVM that was to have far reaching consequences. This was her appearance to an English hermit called Simon Stock, so named because he lived in a tree. Again we have a resonance with very ancient symbolism in that a tree marks the entrance to the portal of initiation. In this instance Our Lady presented Simon with a cloak of the type known as a scapular. That is, a narrow garment that labouring monks used to wear over their habits to prevent them from getting soiled. A confraternity was formed that is still popular among Roman Catholics, although the scapular has shrunk to the form of a medallion. It has been the subject of some contention in the claim that anyone wearing it at their death would be preserved from hell.

The idea of the intercession of the Virgin to protect the sinner from the consequences of sin in an after-world hell plays a dominant role in *The Divine Comedy* of Dante. This masterpiece of the high Middle Ages provides a sequential Mystery system that is the Western equivalent of the highest flights of Tibetan Mahayana Buddhism. Indeed it would be possible to produce a profound synthesis of Eastern and Western symbolic Mysticism by a parallel analysis of *The Divine Comedy* and *The Tibetan Book of the Dead*.

Dante is conducted by Virgil (the embodiment of the highest possible intellectual attainment possible to men) through various forms of hell that are the equivalent of the various hells within the iron mountain in the Buddhist Mount Meru system. The subsequent ascent of Mount Purgatory to the Earthly Paradise is the equivalent of the slopes of Mount Meru that lead to the great palace of the gods at its summit. And the ascent through the Heavens beyond is a similar experience to that of the Buddha-fields of the formless worlds that lead to *Nirvana*.

Dante's poem is a culmination of the revelation of the feminine principle to the medieval mind. This principle had by now expressed itself in many ways. Some of these were to be regarded as heretical or secular, such as the courts of Courtly Love. Others, such as the burgeoning of the Cult of the Blessed Virgin Mary, were considered more theological and orthodox.

In Dante's vision the masculine intellect, even at its highest and most poetic or magical levels, can only go so far in the comprehension of reality, and that is to the external limits of the Earthly Paradise. Therefore when Dante, having traversed the deepest pits of Hell, and climbed the spiral path of Mount Purgatory, comes to the brook that circumscribes the Garden of Eden, he is able to go no further under Virgil's guidance. Virgil can only return to Limbo, the noble but loveless state of the intellect, that can only see the world on its own terms and within its own limitations. To go further the force of love is necessary.

This force is embodied by Beatrice, who expresses not only mortal love but carries the blinding, transfiguring power of divine love as well; that which created the worlds and holds them in being. It is she who meets Dante at the limits of the Earthly Paradise and escorts him through the Heavenly Spheres to the limits of the Uncreate Empyreum beyond the Heavens.

It is in fact she, the embodiment of the feminine principle, who is responsible for the whole Divine Comedy anyway, for it is upon her initiative that Dante, wandering lost in the dark wood of the world, is given the opportunity to embark upon his conducted tour of the inner conditions of the soul.

In fact, in accordance with the most ancient of goddess symbolism, this feminine initiative is threefold. Dante's condition had first been the concern of the Virgin Mary, the noble Lady of Heaven. She calls it to the attention of St Lucia, described as the enemy of all cruelty, and whose very name signifies light. She in turn asks Beatrice, whom he loved in mortal life, to intercede. Beatrice then appears to Virgil, beseeching him to conduct Dante on the first stages of this errand of mercy.

It is not until Virgil has led Dante through the depths of Hell and up the spiral path of the terraces of Mount Purgatory in a form of alchemical or initiation process, that Dante can face the purity and beauty of the Heavenly Beatrice. This is a meeting of great power and significance for it is the moment of the purified soul coming face to face with the reality of divine love after sloughing off the limitations of the vales of illusion.

When Dante finally approaches the verges of the Earthly Paradise he finds it represents the world as it should have been. Sweet gentle breezes blow through beautiful glades in which song birds sing. A clear stream runs under the shady trees at its perimeter and on the further side he sees a maiden gathering flowers. She is singing like one in love, and wending her way like a nymph through the woodland shades.

Woodland nymphs, we may recall, were also associated with the Garden of Hesperides. Indeed they were also associated with the Mysteries of the ancient world, and any who heard the call of their double pipes in the woods knew well to keep well away, for that was the call for the initiates to assemble.

The singing maiden, like an iniatrix of old, bids Dante to look and listen; and through the wood there comes the most beautiful music, running on the shining air. On the far side of the brook a resplendent pageant approaches them. This marks the return of love, the personal presence of Beatrice. It also prepares Dante for his return to the conditions of the Earthly Paradise, long lost.

What is to come is the core of the Mysteries of the Feminine Principle. It is akin to the awakening of the sleeping goddess in naked glory and splendour in *The Chymical Marriage of Christian Rosencreutz*. And also the appearance of the great goddess Isis in all her splendour to the repentant Lucius the ass. Or to the sky-walking dakinis who are the consorts of the highest compassionate buddhas in the Tibetan system. Or to the source of the golden apples of the Hesperides that were the key to the possession of the pure maiden huntress Atalanta. It is therefore not unfitting that at this point the author of the *Divine Comedy* pauses to invoke the virgin Muses on their heights on Mount Helicon, and in particular the Muse Urania. It is she who inspires knowledge of astronomy and heavenly things. The most divine secrets of Love are, in short, held within 'the starry wisdom'.

The interpretation of the symbolic Divine Pageant that then appears strikes even the poetic genius of Virgil dumb. It is better imagined and contemplated therefore, rather than explained.

Seven golden candlesticks precede, akin to the seven lamps mentioned in Exodus XXX that are a part of the symbolic accoutrements of the Ark of Covenant. They are also 'the seven lamps of fire burning before the throne, which are the seven

spirits of God' in Revelation IV. In ancient Eastern esoteric lore
they might be associated with the Seven Rays or seven modes of
divine expression in the solar system. The light from these
candlesticks spreads a rainbow canopy over all that follows.

This includes, first of all, twenty-four ancient men, two by
two, crowned with fleur-de-lys—or formalized lily flowers (the
equivalent of the oriental lotus) that signify mystical wisdom.
They are akin to the twenty-four elders mentioned in Revelation
IV seated about the throne of God, but here they are singing a
hymn in praise of the expression of the feminine principle:
'Blessed art thou amongst the daughters of Adam, and forever
blessed be thy beauty'.

Then follow four magnificent beasts, each with six wings, that
like a peacock's tail are full of eyes. They are crowned with
wreaths, and are described as following the twenty-four elders
as inevitably as star follows star in the whirling heavens. Dante,
despairing of doing justice to a true description of them, refers
the reader to the Vision of Ezekiel. This, in the New English
Bible, reads (Ch. I. v4–13):

> I saw a strong wind coming from the north, a vast cloud with flashes
> of fire and brilliant light about it: and within was a radiance like
> brass, glowing in the heart of the flames. In the fire was the
> semblance of four living creatures in human form. Each had four
> faces and each four wings; their legs were straight, and their hooves
> were like the hooves of a calf, glittering like a disc of bronze. Under
> the wings on each of the four sides were human hands; all four
> creatures had faces and wings, and their wings touched one
> another. They did not turn as they moved; each creature went
> straight forward. Their faces were like this: all four had the face of a
> man and the face of a lion on the right, on the left the face of an ox
> and the face of an eagle. Their wings were spread; each living
> creature had one pair touching its neighbours', while one pair
> covered its body. They moved straight forward in whatever
> direction the spirit would go; they never swerved in their course.
> The appearance of the creatures was as if fire from burning coals or
> torches were darting to and fro among them; the fire was radiant,
> and out of the fire came lightning.

It may be instructive at this point to quote also from the first
eleven verses of Revelations IV:

After this I looked, and there before my eyes was a door opened in heaven, and the voice that I had first heard speaking to me like a trumpet said, 'Come up here, and I will show you what must happen hereafter.' At once I was caught up by the Spirit. There in heaven stood a throne, and on the throne sat one whose appearance was like the gleam of jasper and cornelian; and round the throne was a rainbow, bright as an emerald. In a circle about this throne were twenty-four other thrones, and on them sat twenty-four elders, robed in white and wearing crowns of gold. From the throne went out flashes of lightning and peals of thunder. Burning before the throne were seven flaming torches, the seven spirits of God, and in front of it stretched what seemed like a sea of glass, like a sheet of ice.

In the centre, round the throne itself, were four living creatures, covered with eyes, in front and behind. The first creature was like a lion, the second like an ox, the third had a human face, the fourth was like an eagle in flight. The four living creatures, each of them with six wings, had eyes all over, inside and out, and by day and by night without pause they sang:

Holy, holy, holy is God the sovereign Lord of all, who was, and is, and is to come.

As often as the living creatures give glory and honour and thanks to the One who sits on the throne, who lives for ever and ever, the twenty-four elders fall down before the One who sits on the throne and worship him who lives for ever and ever; and as they lay their crowns before the throne they cry:

Thou art worthy, O Lord our God, to receive glory and honour and power, because thou didst create all things; by thy will they were created, and have their being!

We have quoted this at length to show the magnitude of the honour and glory that is being paid to the one who rides in the chariot in the midst of the procession. It is directly equivalent to that accorded to the Most High God.

The chariot or car might be considered indeed a moving equivalent of the Throne of God. It is indeed of almost indescribable magnificence. It is drawn by a fabulous beast, described as a red and white griffon with golden wings arching so high that their extremities cannot be seen.

As for the carriage, even the light of the sun would look dim beside it. Around one of its two wheels, three maidens are dancing an intricate measure. One of them is red as fire, one green like a precious emerald, and one white as new-fallen snow. About the other wheel are four maidens clad in royal purple, their leader possessing a third eye.

Although common exegesis regards these figures as an allegory of the three Virtues and the four Cardinal Virtues, there is a much deeper esoteric meaning. They represent the feminine expression of the seven rays which are the inner dynamics of the universe, which in the heavens are associated with the Pleiades.

Following the car and the seven dancing maidens are seven aged men. Dante describes them as being seven counterparts of the seven maidens, which in esoteric stellar symbolism equates them with the seven *rishis* of the Great Bear. Instead of garlands of lilies about their heads like the maidens, their brows are wreathed in red roses, so that from a short distance it appears as if their heads are aflame.

With a great thunderclap the whole procession halts, the carriage opposite Dante, and at this moment Dante chooses to compare it with the constellation of the Wain or the Great Bear. This is an important passage esoterically, and indicates a deep knowledge of spiritual star lore, about which very little has been written.

The 'Pointers' of the Great Bear are alluded to in *Esoteric Astrology* by Alice Bailey as major stars of direction. The one nearer the Pole Star (Dubhe) is a focus of the expression of the will of the individual; the one further from the Pole Star (Merak) is the focus of a great reservoir of the energy of Divine Purpose, or the Will of God. The Earthly planetary centre of Shamballah is related to all this, as also those psychic centres in man that concern the spiritual will. Dubhe is the 'pointer' for mankind on the path of the *involution* of consciousness, seeking expression in manifestation. Merak comes into play in guiding the achieved human being into discipleship under the Planetary Hierarchy. And the pattern for the Planetary Hierarchy is to be found in the great star of Isis, Sirius, the Dog Star, in Canis Major.

The griffon-drawn carriage coming to a halt before Dante is an event which seems as pregnant with meaning as if the very heavens themselves had ceased to revolve. The figures about it face toward it. Dante calls them the 'people of truth' and they chant, three times, a phrase from the canticles, 'Come, bride of

Lebanon' (Ch. 4, v 8). The Canticles or Song of Solomon is one book of the Old Testament from which the recognition of the feminine principle has not been excluded.

Then with a cry like to the paeon of praise at the Last Judgment angels arise round the chariot singing. One phrase they sing is adapted from the cries of the multitude when Christ entered Jerusalem in triumph (Matthew XXI: 9); which was a passage from Psalm CXVIII: 26; 'Blessed is he that cometh in the name of the Lord'. In this case the phrase is slightly changed to 'Blessed art *thou* who comest'. This is as if not to proclaim overtly the possibility of a feminine Christ. Indeed how Dante avoided being condemned for heresy remains something of a miracle. The other phrase the angels cry is from a pagan text: 'Oh, give lilies with full hands'. This is from the *Aeniad* VI: 883 of Virgil himself, Dante's guide to this point. Lilies are, of course, the feminine flower, par excellence, in religious symbolism. They are the equivalent of the oriental lotus, and are also associated with the Virgin Mary. The archangel Gabriel is commonly depicted carrying them in paintings of the Annunciation.

Then with flowers showering about her from the angelic hosts there steps from the car one whose coming is likened to the very dawn itself. She is veiled in white, with a cloak of green worn over a dress that is as red as fire. The theological interpretation of these colours seems less appropriate than their relevance to the Isis of Nature—that of a living fire within, clad in a mantle of green vegetation, veiled with white clouds. Above all she is crowned, not with gold, but with olives—the fruit of wisdom, associated with the goddess of wisdom, Pallas Athene, the virgin goddess who arose fully armed from the head of Zeus, the king of the Olympean gods.

At this point of revelation, Virgil, Dante's guide hitherto, the great exemplar of the heights of human intellect, poetic inspiration and magical power, disappears. He can take Dante no further. His instructor from henceforth, who leads him through the heavens, is the great feminine power of Divine Love. This is no theological or platonic abstraction, for she announces herself as a flesh and blood woman. 'Look at me well: truly I am, truly I am Beatrice', the girl whom Dante had loved in Florence.

We will leave this great pageant of the ascent of the soul of man at this point. It has its equivalent in the Buddha-fields high over the City of the Gods in the Mount Meru system of Mahayana Buddhism.

Sufficient has been examined, we trust, to indicate the great power and transforming energy of the feminine principle, in this work of medieval genius. This same principle was known to the ancients under the various forms of the Goddess, and its power and influence continued into the Christian epoch as the image and lore of the Blessed Virgin Mary.

Dante was writing at the beginning of the fourteenth century. At about this time seats of learning, such as Oriel College, Oxford, began to be dedicated to the Virgin. In the fifteenth century there followed the period of great Renaissance paintings of the Madonna, such as Piero della Francesca's *Madonna della Misericord* (1445) and Leonardo da Vinci's *Virgin of the Rocks* (1481–3). And with the coming of the printing press the Office of Our Lady was printed for wide distribution by Guthenburg's successor in 1457.

Another holy house became famous in the beginning of the sixteenth century that rivalled that of Walsingham. This was at Loretto, officially recognized as a place of pilgrimage in 1507. This was the focus of a legend that angels had actually transported the house of the Annunciation through space and time.

With the Reformation abuses of superstition accumulating around such places excited the opposition of reforming bodies. Indeed Henry VIII razed Walsingham to the ground at the Dissolution of the Monasteries in 1538, even though he himself had given generous endowments to it in his youth. Its miraculous statue was taken to London and burned.

Different Protestant bodies took differing lines of reaction according to local and national temperament. The Lutheran Church, for instance, was less rigorous than the barbarous spite that utterly destroyed, in the Lady Chapel at Ely Cathedral in 1539, the two-hundred-year-old carvings of the life and miracles of the Virgin. Had they survived they would have been a most precious spiritual and historical heritage.

There is scope for the analysis of the psychology of group souls to try to identify the cause of such barbarous ferocity that was akin to the vandalism of repressed adolescence. It was in some instances like a reaction to the feminine, or fear of it, welling up from deep levels. This had a strange aftermath in the Puritan areas of East Anglia and New England, with the witch-cults and the paranoid persecution of women as witches. This was almost like a visitation upon a society that could not come to terms with the feminine principle. It had to project it outwards and then persecute it.

However, the Reformation did not completely stamp out the use of images in religious worship. Nor could it for long repress the feminine principle. When abuses are overcome, then genuine expression is free to gain greater recognition. Since then the legends and iconography of the Blessed Virgin Mary have gradually increased in importance and spiritual significance.

Of particular note are the promulgations of the Dogma of the Immaculate Conception in 1854, and of the Assumption of the Blessed Virgin Mary into Heaven, promulgated in 1950. The psychologist C. G. Jung has drawn attention to the psychological implications of these ideas, and it is not without significance that the general movement towards acceptance of the feminine principle in economic, social and political life expression has been gaining impetus. There is still a long way to go, and the movement is not without its unbalanced adherents who bring disrepute through overstatement, but that is common to all human movements for change.

In 1954 the Feast was established of the Blessed Virgin as Queen of Heaven. This is the ultimate recognition of the principle of form, the Earth itself, being as holy as any so called higher state. In its full implication it is the preparation of the New Jerusalem adorned as a Bride.

These are highly metaphysical matters which are beyond the reach of intellectual analysis. We have briefly indicated the increasing realization of the importance of the feminine principle as a consequence of a maturing consciousness of humankind. We have indicated earlier manifestations of this principle in the childhood of the race, and given specific instances of way-showers in the vanguard of general human progress—as depicted in the symbolic images of Dante, the Rosicrucian Brotherhood, and the Mysteries of Isis.

The potential literature for an intellectual study of this is vast. We hope we have provided a few simple pointers on the way. It is however, a 'centering in', rather than a wandering in the labyrinthine fields of intellectual speculation, that is the direct way of truth. The rose blooms at the centre of the Cross. And those who are prepared to contemplate the imagery and take it unto their inmost hearts are the more likely to be met by Beatrice from the triumphal car, and led to places where even the intellectual genius of a Virgil cannot go. To this end we can hardly do better than to survey the body of images that are presented in the Litany of the Blessed Virgin Mary. Any of these images will infinitely repay meditation, contemplation and appropriate acts of symbolic or ritual intention. They may be grouped under the three heads of Mother, Maiden or Virgin, and Queen.

Mother of god, of Christ, of divine grace, most pure, most chaste, inviolate, undefiled, most lovable, most wonderful, of good counsel, of the Creator, of the Saviour.

Virgin most prudent, most venerable, most renowned, most mighty, most merciful, most faithful.
    Mirror of righteousness.
    Seat of wisdom.
    Cause of our joy.
    Spiritual vessel.
    Vessel of honour.
    Wondrous vessel of devotion.
    Mystical rose.
    Tower of David.
    Tower of ivory.
    House of gold.
    Ark of the covenant.
    Gate of heaven.
    Star of the morning.
    Health of the sick.
    Refuge of sinners.
    Consoler of the afflicted.
    Help of Christians.

Queen of Angels, Patriarchs, Prophets, Apostles, Martyrs, Confessors, Virgins, all Saints, conceived without original sin, taken up into heaven, of the most holy Rosary. *Queen of Peace.*

In this last title, Queen of Peace, she shows an aspect of the feminine principle that is akin to a great figure who wanders like a shadow through the early pages of biblical history, the great high priest Melchizedek. His name means 'priest-king' and his title, King of Salem, means King of Peace.

When, in his letter to the Hebrews, the apostle Paul tried to describe something of the eternal nature of Jesus, the Christ, he likened him to a great forerunner in the Hebrew tradition and in fact called him 'an high priest after the order of Melchizedek'.

He went on to say: 'For this Melchizedek, King of Salem, priest of the most high God, who met Abraham returning from the slaughter of the kings, and blessed him; to whom also Abraham gave a tenth part of all; first being by interpretation King of righteousness, and after that also King of Salem, which is, King of Peace; without father, without mother, without descent, having neither beginning of days, nor end of life; but made like unto the Son of God; abideth a priest continually. Now consider how great this man was, unto whom even the patriarch Abraham gave the tenth of his spoils!'

And if we turn from the seventh chapter of the Epistle to the Hebrews to the original reference to Melchizedek in the fourteenth chapter of Genesis, we find that Abram (as he was then named) met this great figure when he was returning from victorious battle with the strange kings who had abducted his brother, Lot. 'And Melchizedek king of Salem brought forth bread and wine: and he was the priest of the most high God.' Thus we see that the central sacraments of the Christian religion are foreshadowed by the acts of this very early priestly figure, Melchizedek.

All we have to go on are these few words in the Bible, for Melchizedek came in such far back and shadowy times that it is very difficult to place any historical accuracy or knowledge around him. Yet he is the source of the Christian sacraments and the core of a deeply significant body of tradition in various mystical schools.

It is something of a marvel that the translators of the Bible, so worried lest anyone should have false doctrine, did not interfere with the great occult facts brought through, for in the Bible there is truly occult summing up of the state and condition in which Melchizedek worked. And of course, St Paul, in spite of the much advertised human failings that he had, was nonetheless a very great mystic as well as a great teacher; and he helped to bring the right teaching through, for he likened Jesus to Melchizedek.

Melchizedek is 'without father, without mother, without descent, having neither beginning of days, nor end of life; but made like unto the Son of God; abideth a priest continually.' The first part of this phrase shows Melchizedek as having all the marks of those great beings who came to teach mankind in ancient days, who, in esoteric teaching, are sometimes called Manus. There are others besides Melchizedek. One of such is Narada, of very early Atlantean times, who is said to have been opposed to the Divine plane for humanity which decreed the differentiation of mankind into two sexes. Another is Oannes, or Dagon, of ancient Babylonia, but Melchizedek is probably the greatest. Each of these Manus was responsible for laying down the pattern for a new race or civilization of humanity.

Such great beings were of course, 'without father, without mother, without descent', in the human sense of those terms. And also they had 'neither beginning of days, nor end of life'. This means that they had no actual dense body, as we know the word, but were able to build up a certain amount of physical appearance and then disappear, to appear somewhere else, and so on. This would have been a very strong kind of 'etheric projection', strong enough to appear to the men of those times—who had in fact a certain degree of natural clair-voyance—and which might be compared to the materialization of forms in certain spiritualist circles nowadays. It must be remembered though that there is a great difference between the manifestation of a recently deceased human being and the appearance of one of these great beings, just as there is a very great difference between the communications of the average spiritualist meeting and the teachings that come from a genuine contact with one of the Inner Plane Adepti or Masters. And even Masters, being human, albeit advanced humans, can hardly be compared with such beings as Melchizedek. St Paul says of

Melchizedek that he 'abideth a priest continually'. He abideth—he stays, he waits, he endures—continually—going on all the time, in unbroken sequence or extent, connected throughout in space and time, without break or interruption. Thus he is available to be contacted by all who seek him now, as he ever was, even in the days of Abraham.

In this there is a true and real connection between him and the Christ, as indicated by St Paul, for Jesus said: 'Behold, I am with you always, even unto the end of the world,' and 'Whenever two or three are gathered together in my name, there am I in the midst of them.'

As Dion Fortune trenchantly remarked, any who seek after direct experience of occult powers and esoteric teachings have only to go on their knees and earnestly invoke the Christ and they may find they get all they ever expected, and probably a great deal more than they bargained for! It is strange, in a way, that for many would-be occultists, there is apparently a psychological block against even attempting to make inner contact with these two great priests of the Most High God.

Tradition tells us that Melchizedek brought to the Mysteries three mighty symbols, which represent his gifts to man, and which come, even as he did, in the beginning, from Venus, the morning and evening star. These three great gifts are capable of infinite results to applied meditation. They are symbols holding symbols and again holding symbols, which in the end resolve into the great Truth which has no symbol.

Teachers from Venus, for there were others, brought always the symbol of food and growth. Thus one of his symbols is wheat, by which people live. It is a source of nourishment, spiritual as well as physical, for in the cycle of grain, being cut down, and buried, only to rise again, are the teachings of all the great religions and Mystery schools. In it are the two great principles of life, the Law of Cycles and the Law of Sacrifice.

Melchizedek brought also the honey bee, which is again the symbol of the hive, of the dedicated and cultured community. Thus it represents also the New Jerusalem in which every human being is destined to be a cell. The six-sided cell of the honey bee is also representative of the six-rayed star, the Star of David, whose esoteric meaning is the perfect union of lower and higher man, for it is a conjunction of two triangles.

The third symbol is the strange vegetable-like mineral, asbestos, which signifies the spiritual incorruptible man which is impervious to the vicissitudes of the world just as the asbestos cannot be burned by the fire.

In paintings and sculptures (and there is a particularly evocative stone image of him at Chartres) Melchizedek is shown holding a chalice, and the chalice is another great symbol of the holier side of Venus. It is also a symbol of the Christ; and it is also a symbol of the Holy Grail. There is, indeed, a legend that the Grail fell from Venus as an emerald from Lucifer's crown, and was carved into the shape of a chalice. In the Chartres statue of Melchizedek, there is a stone within the chalice.

Some idea of the magnitude of being of such a one as Melchizedek can perhaps be obtained by considering him as an aspect of the Lord of the World, the Spirit or Regent of the planet Earth. He has been called the Father of Humanity, and in terms of Eastern inspired esoteric teaching he is the equivalent of what is there called Sanat Kumara, which, broadly translated, means 'the eternal youth'.

It is customary, in religious and esoteric symbolism, to denote great wisdom by the appearance of great age. Thus beings such as Christian Rosencreutz, Melchizedek, the Ancient of Days, are pictured as old men. God and the regents of heaven are, however, existent in a timeless condition, and we should ever remember this and not let our symbolism delude us into thinking of wisdom in terms of senility. In the realms beyond the temporal limitations of the physical universe, all is continually renewing, eternally vibrant, ever young.

By the same token we should not allow ourselves to be limited or misled by sexual conventions of symbolism any more than those of age. All that we have said of Melchizedek, the Great High Priest, has an equivalent in what might be called the Great High Priestess, a concept almost totally lacking in the paternalist traditions of the Bible as it has come down to us, although perhaps, in somewhat disguised form as the Queen of Sheba who visited the Priest-King Solomon.

Such a figure is represented in the Tarot. The Tarot symbol of the High Priestess is a figure in blue draperies, seated between two pillars, a veil behind her, upon her lap a book or scroll, and the moon and the suggestion of swirling waters at her feet.

She represents the great figure of ancient mythology and religion who had human qualities as well as divine, the goddess Isis, Isis Ourania, Queen of Heaven, crowned in the highest and enthroned in the hearts of men. She who was also known as the Lady of Wild Things, Our Lady of Nature, the Lady of the Moon and the Night Sky. She who sorrowed and searched for dismembered Osiris, who knew bitter grief and searing disappointments.

We can see in her the same figure that has been built up for us in Mary the Mother of Jesus. Both of them have been known as the Mother of God, the Star of the Sea, the Gate of Heaven. And as Isis had the grief of searching for the body of her consort Osiris, the Divine King, who had been betrayed and killed and mutilated, so is Mary the Mater Dolorosa, the Sorrowful Mother, whose heart was pierced with the Swords of Anguish, who stood at the foot of the Cross and received into her arms the dead and mutilated body of her son.

This is a human figure who can understand all sorrows, help all weaknesses, who watched with eyes dimmed with tears the approaching death of Jesus. She is, as it were, the human aspect of the Queen of Heaven. As Jesus is sometimes called the Lord of the Personality, so might Mary be called its Mother, as exemplified in her other titles of Refuge of Sinners, Comforter of the Afflicted, Mother of Mercy. To her, standing in her desolation at the foot of the Cross, the Saviour gave as a son his beloved disciple, and in so doing made her the protectress of all humanity. Thus she whom we know as the Queen of Heaven, Ever Virgin, Ever Mother, is, as well, the Sorrowful Mother of the Gospels, and through the human we can reach up to the divine.

From this, we can see how the Christian religion, the Christian Myth, can be added to the other great myths. Now it is said that a myth is one of those stories which expresses in dramatic form a universal need in our souls. It is the dramatization of an experience of the soul through which man can see himself exemplified. No true myth is a fancy, an idle tale to while away a leisure hour. They are very far otherwise, particularly for those who can consciously perceive their inner worth.

In this sense Christianity is a myth; not 'only a myth', but the story of a sequence of events so true in their essence that the story of history attains the dignity and fundamental truth of a myth, a great universal myth. Religions are formulae for the use of man, who is created in the image and likeness of God. They are most suitable for our progress and guidance, but even as formulae are many, each best suited to a particular purpose, so are there many cults. Religions and mythological formulae grow as knowledge grows, the knowledge of the great eternal principles which are the Nature of God, and therefore of man.

But there is no need to specify whether the great figure of the second Tarot Trump, esoterically called 'The Priestess of the Silver Star', is a 'Christian' or a 'Pagan' figure. She is eternal and has descended in some way through all the major religious systems, whether as Demeter sorrowing for her daughter, or Ishtar walking through the Seven Hells for her lover, or Mary watching her son die. It is the same figure.

When Christianity took the place of the more ancient creeds the figure of Mary, the Mother of Jesus, gradually evolved into a great form of divine tragedy, but in another degree, because Mary represents the most spiritualized essence of all these goddess tragedies. The sense of sorrow is at a more highly spiritualized and supernal level.

This is where the idea of the Mother of the Lord Jesus may have a great deal more teaching for us at this phase of our civilization than have the pagan forms. She represents the sorrow that comes to the more civilized and evolved type of mind, the modern mind. She stands for that particular aspect of the Great Mother whose sorrow can take more actual part in, have greater reality for, the modern mind.

Sorrow is a divine and potent thing. However hard it may sound, it is suffering and sorrow that are usually the only things to make the soul grow. We call it 'learning by experience'. And the man who cannot feel sorrow is in a bad way, there is no life in him until he can be unhappy and face and accept unhappiness as a necessary part of life, in himself and others. If he cannot do this he is self-anaesthetized, or psychologically deadened.

So, as it is often only on the ladder of sorrow that the soul can mount to God, we can see how important it is for the soul's contemplation and health to have a mighty figure of Eternal Sorrow as an archetype or pattern. And this very great figure knows the extent of grief in every type of human nature. She knows that it must work its end, that it must teach man's nature certain things, that it helps a person to bear a thing that somehow must be borne; and sometimes to watch another who has gone through more.

Mary had gone through a great deal more. Many mothers have known their sons to die, and seen them die, but not such a son as Mary's and not for such a reason.

In this sorrow there are many aspects to be found. There is the power that comes from pain after it has been realized and assimilated and understood; a power like no other power. There is the wisdom that has probed the depths of the soul and understands its own soul—and therefore other souls—for nothing probes the soul and makes a person understand himself like suffering, whether the suffering be spiritual, mental, emotional or physical.

Thus we have the Power and the Wisdom of what is sometimes called the Purple ray, or Ray of Love, exemplified by the great image of the Sorrowing Mother, 'Stabat Mater Dolorosa', as she stands in the midst of the purple light.

Popular Roman Catholic piety has sentimentalized Mary too much, so that many modern people are turned back from the rather naive and even foolish things that have been written and painted. It may be well, therefore, to turn to the great school of early Greek Christian art, and consider that form of Mary, archaic and stern, sometimes terrible, far more the great transcendental figure than the Italian women who have been made Madonnas. The great, dark eyed, strong type of woman wearing her black Byzantine robes with golden stars decorating the background produces far more the figure of what Mary was really to become.

There are many legends of her, though very little is told of her in the Bible. Her character is revealed very little, but that little tells a great deal. One of the things that is most striking and important about her is the quality of silence. She who knew wonderful and terrible inner experiences far beyond the knowledge and experience of any ordinary woman—and who had the inner wisdom and power to keep such things to herself. Think of the innate power and wisdom of that very young Jewish girl who confided in no one, who continued to lead, apparently, an ordinary life, looking after her own household, seeing her own women relations and friends occasionally, watching with a terrible knowledge the mission of her son, knowing what the final achievement in the world would be, and doubtless knowing at least some part of the other achievements in other worlds as well.

Here then we have the human aspect of that tremendous tragic figure of whatever name we like, individually, to give her—Demeter, Ishtar, Isis, Mary, Priestess of the Silver Star. She is still the Dark Mother, still the Queen of the Potent Silence, the Realizer of Tragedy, the results of which are to cleanse and purify the soul. Those of us who have a grief, and who endeavour to go on as best we can carrying that burden within us, will gain strength from the Dark Virgin Mother, for she is mighty, she is a part of God, just as she is a part of every human being.

There is another archetypal feminine Tarot Trump, the Empress, that reflects yet another facet of the feminine principle, and one which is particularly important to us in this day and age.

This is not as the Queen, Empress or High Priestess of the high Cosmic Spaces or Deep Heaven—but of the planet Earth. That is, as representing the body of Elemental consciousness that goes to make up the material sphere upon which we live and move and have our being. A more common way of describing her would be as Mother Nature. Or in more esoteric terms as the Planetary Being (or in some works as the Planetary Entity).

There is a great deal to be gained from coming to some conscious awareness of the reality of this vast pool of Elemental Consciousness which we call the Planetary Being. Yet it is difficult to describe such a great being as a real thing, for it is not readily apparent to the human mind except in some forms of psychism or clairvoyance.

When there is a strong contact made with it by a human being, a tremendous fear can arise, a fear which is akin to the fear of open spaces. It is a very terrible thing, and some would call it a form of deep hysteria—or Pan-ic terror. But it does not matter what we may care to call this awe-ful awareness, the fact is that it is a real thing, very real on its own plane and very real in the feeling it can give to a human being.

Nevertheless, as in the legends of Pan (and the forces of the Planetary Being are closely linked to the mythology of Pan), those who are truly attuned to the earth do not feel the fear. Those who feel it are those not so attuned, who are frightened of natural things and who have no real love or need of Nature, for underlying the Planetary Being is the great Essence from which primeval Nature bubbled up into the Earth itself and into the instinctual side of man. It is precisely this factor which lives with and in primitive man very strongly.

This primeval force is by no means evil—save when the minds of men make it so. It has, indeed, something of the reflection of God the Father within it. Thus is Pan conceived of as a male being. But there is equally a passive or feminine side to it as shown in the figure of the Empress and her Venus symbolism. In all great natural forces there is a 'positive' and a 'negative', a 'male' and a 'female' side.

The positivity of the male force is well known about under various terms such as the 'libido', 'hyle', 'life-force' and so on. The negative female force is perhaps less understood. It can be very terrible and strong—for it can hold itself open to bring through and to mould forces from far off spheres. It is certainly by no means a timid, resigned and inferior force as is sometimes so wrongly and indeed so ridiculously thought.

If we want to think of the Planetary Being in the best way, we must think of it as a holy being; and also as one which is, in a way, a parent to us, a Father/Mother type, whom it is our duty to cherish, to help, and to some extent to guide, for new aspects of being have come to us in the course of our evolution through the development of mind. But the Planetary Being has no mind.

It is often very difficult for those who have no great deal of esoteric awareness or experience to visualize a mindless entity; and in this case a mindless entity with tremendous force—absolutely pure, good and true on its own level, but from a rational point of view, ruthless, or even antagonistic. For it works through great will and instinct but not through mind or through any considerations of a mental nature.

The beings who are closer to it than man, the Elementals, also work in this way. They are pure and blind forces too, for the most part, with no mind; absolutely holy, pure and good in their own law—which they do not seek to break. It is mankind who breaks the laws. We, mankind, who have been guilty of breaking laws throughout all our evolution. And indeed one could say it is part of the human type of development. Man must be for ever a rebel and for ever breaking laws, because only by breaking certain laws can he develop! This is, at one and the same time, the blessing and the curse of what we call mind.

But we are not here concerned with issues of moral philosophy. We are striving for an awareness of the real relationship that exists between the subtler forces of the Earth and ourselves. Really it is a feeling of love for the Earth that is necessary, an awareness of nearness and a sense of relation-ship—even for the most city bound of us. For in this sense of relationship and of love there will not be room for any fear—or any evil. It is only through fear that evil first came to the world, and still comes, to this very day.

Long ago it was said that at the time of the Crucifixion, a strange voice was heard calling out across the seas: 'Great Pan is dead', and this was thought to mean that all the old gods and all their ways had been killed because the One True God had come. This is not quite accurate—though there is truth in it. Pan was not dead, but something connected with 'death' did come to the Earth. It changed.

It changed through the tremendous energy which came to Earth two thousand years ago. It did actually change within itself, even actually in its own nature. There was something even in the Earth itself, after this great event, a little bit more approaching to spirituality than there had been before. After the Crucifixion the spiritual factors which came from the Christ force in connection with the Earth entered into the structure of the Earth, and the Earth began, very slowly and very subtly, to change, and to go upwards to a course where it shall become a fully developed planet—'when the Kingdom comes to Earth'.

The Crucifixion was as a 'pause' in a great cycle, like the 'pause' one gets in any cycle when the nadir or zenith of an arc is rounded. On the lesser cycle of the year one finds these 'pauses' at two points—at the Summer and the Winter Solstice. And in the cycle of each day there can be detected by those who are sensitive, in the very early morning and between two and three in the afternoon, a very curious type of stillness. This curious feeling, a curious sense of rest, or silence, or stopping, is called 'the pause in nature'. And so are there similar pauses in epochs and evolutions; and the coming of the Christ marked one of them—possibly the greatest in human experience.

Since that event, Great Pan is changed. He is not dead. Were he dead then the Earth itself would be dead, for the living Pan is the Planetary Being, though the Planetary Being is by no means entirely described in the mythology and pagan conception of Pan. In many ways the Tarot Empress or various goddess or feminine mythological images are a more appropriate form.

There is, in the Planetary Being, a tremendous primeval urge for unity and reunion with its own children—and these children include mankind. Indeed, mankind can help the Planetary Being more than any other kind of terrestrial life can, for man has within himself all levels of being, from the primitive instinctual (which relates closest to the Planetary Being), to the spiritual (towards which, in its dim way, the Planetary Being aspires). Primitive man was, and is, very close to the Planetary Being, as are the animal kingdoms—and a comparison of the grace and vitality of the animal and the primitive with that of the average sedentary urbanized man shows that there is much to be gained from retaining this link with the Planetary Being. It is a source of vitality and health and correct bodily functioning.

But the link is not made intellectually. One will never contact the Earth if one is always in a process of thought. One must feel and wish and will towards these things. It is not exactly prayer. Prayer is a lifting of the mind up to God. But here we are not concerned with lifting the mind to God in Heaven, but with extending the heart towards and down to the Planetary Being—who is potentially God in Earth. And though the Planetary Being is greater than man, it is less than man also—and man can bring it far towards a spiritual growth.

Even as with the Elementals, where, according to tradition, a man—if he is himself of the right esoteric stature—can educate an Elemental Being—so it is with that vast 'generating Elemental', the Planetary Being of Earth. Though in this case one man cannot help and educate the Planetary Being fully, but all men can—and must. This is the true meaning of Evolution. We ourselves grow, and contribute growth to that which first brought us forth.

This awareness of responsibility is particularly important for those who aspire to open up the deeper levels of themselves in esoteric or similar work. The more so since the growth of urban civilization and the development of the concrete mind have tended to atrophy the imaginative capacity, through which the divine intention functioning through sensory life can be the easier perceived than by intellectual philosophizing. Thus man no longer strives to apprehend the work of God and to adore the Creator through the instincts and animal nature. He cuts himself off from the deep parental love of the Earth Mother.

In this respect the 'higher' nature of man has much to learn from the personality in the world. And many attracted towards occultism or the enclosed orders of religion are not necessarily 'advanced' souls—but souls who cannot bring themselves to accept and assimilate the experience of the instincts and lower emotions through life in the world. So while the worldly personality should all the time be listening in to the higher nature, whose promptings are usually called 'the voice of conscience', the higher nature has also the task of adjusting itself to the ever changing conditions of ordinary human life. If this were better understood many tragedies could be avoided. For instance, a man may have such a strong link with his higher nature that the pressure of conscience is so strong that he feels his own line of action *must* be right—whatever the cost. Though this may often be lauded as heroism or sanctity it is more often than not fanaticism and bigotry and a travesty of real human values.

So while 'spirituality' and 'the voice of conscience' are very valuable things, there is a world of difference between a spiritual nature operating blindly and ruthlessly after the manner of Torquemada, the founder of the Spanish Inquisition, who tortured souls in order, as he thought, to 'save' them, and spiritual values put into action in the world through the mediation of human love and compassion. So it is not merely a question of the purity or strength of the spiritual force which can be contacted by a soul, but also the means by which this force is applied—and this brings in considerations of relationship with others.

Considerations of relationship grow more important, not less, as evolutionary or spiritual growth is attained, and many experience much difficulty because of this. The personality may be a dedicated and willing instrument but the difficulties raised by a higher nature learning to function rightfully through human channels can be very great. It is a question of taking responsibility for one's effect upon others—and these others extend beyond the frontiers of the human kingdom. They extend to God in Heaven on the one hand—and on the other to his creation in Earth, the Planetary Being, and all the other lives, animal or Elemental, that have the destiny to share the planet with us. It is up to us to endeavour to make that destiny, not a horror, but a blessing.

One way is, as we have tried to indicate in this book, by the equilibration of the Elements within, and the cultivation of the civilizing influence of the Eternal Feminine at its many levels, from heights of Heaven to depths of Earth, with the mediation of human love between.

Part Seven:
The Initiation of the Earth

We began this book with instruction on how to build a magic circle. And having built that circle, how to equilibrate the forces of the watch-towers of the Elements so that the rose of the expressed spirit could grow at their interchange, in the centre of the encircled cross. Through the centre of the concourse of elemental forces the mighty spiritual forces of the Divine Feminine are expressed.

We now give a pattern for all who aspire to put into effect the expression of the feminine principle. Seldom is work of this nature given out but the urgency is great and the issues profound. It needs all the active esoteric participants in the world today that can be found.

The need is for those of esoteric ability, experience, breadth of vision and goodwill to use their talents in a dynamic and positive way. To bridge the gap, the yawning gulf, that presently lies between the stars in the heavens and the stars within the Earth—between the crystals of the inner Earth and the jewels of the Madonna that are set in the splendour of the heavens. And to realize that these are not terms of an overheated poetic fancy, but images of a reality more solid than our everyday world of dreams and illusions, unconscious projections and wish-fulfilment fantasies.

This work requires another dimension of consciousness. This dimension can be reached through the active use of imagination. It is not the same as the imagination. But through this God-like and God-given creative faculty, subjective fancy may give place to objective perception of a greater reality, that complements the physical.

It requires also a breadth of vision and largeness of soul. Those who revere nature and the natural world, including its inner aspects, must strive toward a perception of those great spiritual forces that transcend nature. And those whose hearts are in the transcendental must reach in love toward the natural world and the deep powers that lie within it, the Elementals, the archetypes and the gods, man-made or otherwise.

The meeting point and fulcrum of this mighty axis between Deep Heaven and Deep Earth lies in the human heart. The human heart has, in potential, the capacity to contain all, however mean and miserable its capacity may seem to be as reflected in the state of the world, wherein man's inhumanity to man makes countless thousands mourn, to say nothing of the animal and other dependent creations at the mercy of his 'priesthood'.

Let us, then, build our magic circle, but now in the three dimensions of space instead of a ground plan that embraces only two. Our work must reach upward to the deeps of the heavens and downwards to the heart of the Earth.

Visualize your magic circle as described in the first section of this book, with its four Elemental quarters and its central altar point.

Now remove it from its abstract setting. See it in relation to a sacred site of your choice. This may be one of the ancient megalithic circles that abound or be a modern place of worship. The pagan and the Christian, and indeed all other religions of humankind, are encompassed in this work. Any place that is, or has been, set aside for human contact with numinous realities, however inadequately expressed or conceived, is a power point, a centre for a magic circle whose circumference, in potential, embraces the universe.

Ancient churches and abbeys, in that through time they have channelled the devotions and aspirations of our ancestors—back to the remotest times when the site may have been but a grove on a holy hill—are of particular value and importance for those who can work with them, even if some have been occluded by ancient or modern ignorance. The power of some of these old sites was diverted from spiritual and inner Earth ends by ecclesiastical and political ambitions of some of our forebears.

Hence the evidence we see of great splendours in stone falling into decay. Nonetheless the original pure source of power may be felt and seen shining through as the fountainheads are unblocked.

Build, then, your magic circle over a site of your choice. It is sufficient to have visited it, with some care and devotion. The contact will have been made by this physical pilgrimage and subsequent inner work can then be conducted from far away, or in your own home.

Having built the circle to embrace the ground plan of your selected site, see the circle, with its four cardinal points and its central altar, rise into the air, so that it takes its station high in the sky above the site. Define the circumference of the circle by visualizing free standing pillars around it, of any manageable number, say seven between each quarter, but there is no need to be too precise or pedantic about it.

Be aware of the four-fold dynamic of the Quarters, and at each Quarter see a simple stone altar, with a small ritual fire upon it, standing between two of the pillars to form an Elemental gate. See the central altar take the form of a glowing, flaming brazier or tripod. From the quarters see bands of light and power flow forth across the floor of the temple to meet at the central altar/brazier, so that a pattern of a rose cross is made, the central fire taking the place of the central rose upon the cross. Indeed, it may be conceived as a red rose of fire. (See Figure 4.)

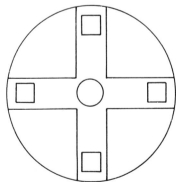

Figure 4

Now see the central fire/rose fill like a cup and overflow with red and with crystal clear liquid, like wine and water, which at times, in its confluence, shimmers like liquid gold. See this liquid overflow from the heart of the temple into the four triangular shaped spaces that are formed between the arms of the Elemental cross. Then see these red, crystal clear, and shimmering gold streams flowing down from the floor of the temple toward the earth in four great, gradually converging, roughly triangular columns. They penetrate the surface of the Earth, encompassing the sacred site as they pass.

At a hidden point within the Earth's core, below the site, they converge, and from the point of their convergence streams of force return that rise to meet the four ends of the arms of the cross in the temple overhead. From each of the four descending columns two upward rays ascend, one to each Quarter point on either side of the original triangular space. Thus twice as much power ascends as descended. See now a cup of water appear on each of the four Elemental altars beside the ritual fires.

A similar pattern of flow may now be seen to build above the temple, with a convergence point high in the heavens. The whole sequence thus gives a geometric form that is similar to an elongated octohedron. (See Figure 5.)

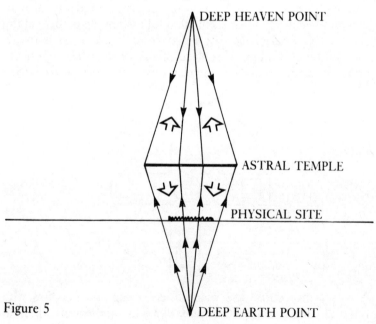

Figure 5

At the point of entry at the surface of the earth around the physical sacred site you may see some of the liquid force flow outward in various directions toward other sites. These lines of force are orderly and straight. And from these secondary sites they flow on again, but now running like golden rivers instead of straight canals, or like veins or arteries, some large some small, fructifying the land and all who live on it with their spiritual and elemental force.

Realize now that the lower point of the octohedron is in fact a gateway to the Underworld forces of the Earth, and that it is as the opening to a cavern that leads ultimately to the secrets of the centre of the Earth.

Be aware, within that hollow and hallowed place, of a feminine figure who represents the under-Earth forces of blood, land, sea, sap, the ancestors, the elemental generating powers, the form givers, Mother Earth herself. This may present itself in a variety of ways—from a fish or serpent-tailed woman to the sleeping Lady Venus of the Rosicrucian vault, from the white and green clad faery queen to one of the Black Madonnas associated with the crypts of certain cathedrals.

Similarly, realize the top of the upper point of the octohedron to be a gateway to the heavens. See a great shining cosmic feminine figure, who, like the figure below, may appear in one of a variety of forms. It could be as Dante's Beatrice stepping from the triumphal carriage; or Astraea, the star maiden of the heavens; or the Blessed Virgin crowned in glory. She is the polar complement and cosmic equivalent of the Lady within the Earth. Isis Urania in polar conjunction with Isis of Nature. The Queen of Heaven in relation to the Sorrowing Mother beneath the Cross.

As these figures form be aware of the power of the Lady of the Heavens flowing downward through the central point of the temple to meet with the upward flowing forces from the Lady beneath the Earth. These forces continue in their polar direction so that there is a complete blending of their currents. Then one is aware, as a climax to the working, that the figures have interchanged. The figure of the Earth Maiden is triumphant in the Heavens, and that of the Star Maiden is radiant, deep within the Earth.

Hold this vision for as long as you will. Then see the figures

slowly resume their former positions; although after this
interchange you realize that nothing will ever be quite the same
as it was before. A great cross-fertilization and sanctification has
taken place.

The upper and lower gates slowly close. The upper and lower
pyramids shrink to their former size, and then revert to the
simple two dimensional circular temple in the sky. Draw your
consciousness back into your daily surroundings, and go about
your daily round content that you have helped to perform an act
of high magic that will help the Earth to shine forth its ultimate
cosmic deity.

A similar type of working can be effected inside a sacred
building. In a typical structure this may best be conceived at the
cross point of transept with nave.

Here, however, simply visualize a golden circle with a rose
cross at each quarter. The golden arms of these four
equal-armed crosses can be visualized to reach one toward the
other so that a circular band of golden light is formed. And then
also their upper and lower arms similarly extend and meet at a
central point overhead and beneath the floor in an interlocking
three-ring system. (See Figure 6.)

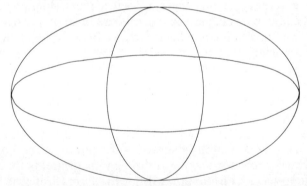

At the centre of this golden network see a point of diamond
and ruby light, with flashes of gold. It grows in size and power
until it becomes a mighty gem. This jewel may grow to
encompass the whole of the spherical figure, and then may be
seen to pulsate, like a beating heart. At the same time it may
transform from one type of Platonic solid to another—to and
from octohedron and cube, dodecahedron and icosohedron, or

as a continually reversing pair of tetrahedra. However, the sense of spiritual and organic life is more important than the geometrics. The colours may also vary according to the site or time of year, month or day.

Once again, above and below this pulsing figure see the Star Maiden and the Earth Maiden—perhaps most appropriately as star cloaked and crowned Madonna of the Immaculate Conception, the moon at her feet, at the height; and a dark robed or black Madonna, as in the crypt at Chartres, below. Again, see and feel the interchange.

The justification for performing this type of working in churches and abbeys should perhaps be emphasized. In ancient, pre-Christian times, wise men understood how the stars and planets influenced the metals and crystals of Earth. Some Earth sites were indeed magnetized to a particular metal or crystalline stone, and by this means became a centre for the dispersal of this influence or an adjunct to a larger site or centre. Lines of travel for this influence ran between sites, linking with other centres, and not only with other centres upon Earth but also starwards.

At many of these centres churches or abbeys came to be built, they themselves receiving a living charge from the lines, and transmuting the influences according to the abilities and understanding of the churchmen. Some transmuted the influences well, so that they became great seats of learning and teaching. Others were blocked by lack of understanding, or became centres of power only, the power being contained at its source and not fed into the living Earth and its people.

It may be thought that the earthly church was unlikely to have had any sympathy with these ancient forces and that it would have cut off, stamped out, or buried 'pagan' influences of this kind; but throughout the history of mankind, whether conquest be cultural or physical, local and national religions have been absorbed and incorporated rather than cut off completely.

At the beginning of Christianity's influence the churchmen were an integral part of the land. And their churches were at first no more than what we would call huts. They lived in a natural fashion in the earth, utilizing cave, rock and tree for their first shelters, building their wattle and daub churches from growing tree and plain earth. They partook directly of Earth, understood it, and were very much part of it, though carrying a mighty spirit within them, and able to link their own spirit with the spirit of Christ and the Godhead.

They were spirit and earth in combination and their early churches were also thus. Their design is remembered for all time in the later great stone edifices filled with column and vaulting, like a great stone forest indeed. Vine or ivy leaves, and oak, and other references to the early shelters of Christians abound in church decoration.

Abbeys later also gave much time to the tilling and cultivation of the soil, to fishing and other natural pursuits of man. As so often happens however, the reason for this work on the land, that is, close contact with God's earth, a great gift, was forgotten, and changed to the pursuit of wealth for the foundation itself, so concentrating power at the source again.

As time proceeded, the knowledge and understanding of the holy use of these lines deteriorated and personal motive overcame spiritual intention. Original guide lines were lost and overlaid, many churches even being built to *stop* the influence of power lines rather than to transmute their energies.

Already some awareness of these things is being revived. Men and women of great hope and idealism have begun the release of the stopped or diverted streams. Mainly the power is simply redirected into the Earth again, for most people assume that these Earth lines belong solely to the Earth. Much is accomplished by those who direct the unstopped energies into the 'grid' of lines. Better still, a very few are able to link the power lines to the physical heavens through star lore. And there are yet others, even fewer, who try to link the lines with the Godhead and thus bring about the 'spiritual' rebirth of the planet.

This is the real 'craft lore' that is needed to help the travailing Earth. It is also the real 'churchmanship' that is needed. God created the Earth as well as the Church and the two are not irreconcilable. The great divorce is only in the narrow minds and constricted hearts of men and women.

The wisdom of the heart is all important. For wisdom is unbalanced and distorted when held only at the intellectual level. The silver wisdom of the head must be changed to the golden wisdom of the heart by the warmth of human love.

Tend the fires of love and understanding most carefully, for without the glow of their light and warmth there is not only no wisdom to be had, there is no point in having the wisdom at all.

The greater vision of unity lies in the transformations of the Goddess, the dancer at the heart of the rose. This is a mystery to be found also in the legends of the Holy Grail and the secret of the jewel in the head of the alchemical toad. That which fell from the crown of the fallen Son of the Morning.

Reflect upon these deep things. And thus may the wisdom of the stars shine in your brow, the grail of love flow from your heart, the waters of life encompass your loins, and the stones of Earth support your feet. This is the image and function of redeemed humankind, the new Adam and new Eve, conjoined in the new Heaven and the new Earth, the new Avalon where the green apples have turned to gold.

Index